# City Dog
## Greater Philadelphia

more help with your pet from

RONNIE
SELLERS
PRODUCTIONS
PORTLAND, MAINE

Published by Ronnie Sellers Productions, Inc.
81 West Commercial Street, Portland, Maine 04101
For ordering information:
(800) 625-3386 Toll Free
(207) 772-6814 Fax
Visit our Web site: www.rsvp.com • E-mail: rsp@rsvp.com

Publishing Director: Robin Haywood
Managing Editor: Mary Baldwin
Production Artists: Kathy Fisher, Charlotte Smith, Nicole Cyr

ISBN: 13: 978-1-56906-970-7
ISBN 10: 1-56906-970-0

**Editor:** Cricky Long
**Content Manager:** Bryce Longton
**Cover Design:** Carol Salvin
**Icon Illustrations:** Bill Kheel
**Interior Design:** Jennifer Ciminillo
**Fact Checker:** Cristina Markarian
**Philadelphia Writers:** Christy Barr,
Kathryn D'Imperio, Marjorie Dorfman,
Marie Fowler, Sara Lebo, Charyn Pfeuffer,
and Kristie Willis

## City Dog

P.O. Box 805
Middleburg, VA 20118
(540) 687-3465 (phone)
www.citydog.net

The purpose of the guidebook is to inform and to entertain. Every effort was
made to ensure that all information contained in this guidebook was accurate
and up-to-date at the time of publication. However, the writers, editor, and City
Dog Publishing, LLC shall have neither liability nor responsibility to any person
or entity with respect to any loss or damage caused, or alleged to have been
caused, directly or indirectly, by the information contained in this book. It is
recommended that you call ahead to confirm business information.

# Contents

# Introduction

*Think of what a place this world could be if only we would all be the people our dogs think we are.*

*City Dog*, the urban dog-o-phile's personal 411 to all things dog, is unique. It is the only dog guide singularly devoted to helping city-dwellers find the dog-care resources they need. This is not a book about people-places that permit dogs, but rather a book about places that are specifically *for* dogs.

The purpose of this guidebook is to help you make your dog the happiest and healthiest he can possibly be.

*City Dog's* A-to-Z directory includes not only the address, phone number, hours of operation, and payment information for each listing, but also an original review of each business. This means you can get the inside scoop, without having to make a personal visit. A service that one dog owner may deem essential might seem utterly frivolous to another. *City Dog* has covered it all. So please, take from this guidebook what you need, use what works for you, and consider the rest entertainment.

## CITY DOG PICKS

What makes a business a City Dog Pick?

Making a business a City Dog Pick is our way of recognizing companies that truly stand out for their exceptional services, products, and/or unique offerings. These businesses do not necessarily offer the most expensive or lavish products or services. However, their products or services are almost certainly a great value.

# Legend

For those of you who don't like to read the fine print,
we have created icons to make it easy for you to see
at a glance who offers what services.

Alternative
Products/Services

Anesthesia-
Free Teeth
Cleaning

Animal Hospitals
& Vet Clinics

Cat Services/
Products Available

City Dog Picks

Dog
Boarding

Dog
Day Care

Dog
Grooming

Dog Hikes &
Socials

Dog Parks
& Trails

Dog
Training

Dog Walking/
Pet Sitting

Dog-centric
Resources

Low-Cost
Vaccination
Clinics

On-Site
Pet Adoptions

Pet-Supply
Stores

Photography/
Paintings

Poop-Removal
Service

Self-Serve Dog
Grooming

Shuttle
Service

$ = Inexpensive
$$ = Average
$$$ = Expensive

## NOTES

Be sure to call to confirm when or what services are offered.

| | | |
|---|---|---|
| | Anesthesia-Free Teeth Cleaning | Teeth cleaning may be only brushing, or it may include the more comprehensive scaling. |
| | City Dog Pick | Making a business a City Dog Pick is our way of recognizing companies that truly stand out for their exceptional services, products, and/or unique offerings. These businesses do not necessarily provide the most expensive or lavish products/services. However, what they do offer is almost certainly a great value. |
| | Dog Hikes & Socials | For a dog hike & social, someone comes to collect dogs – yours and others'– and take them on a walk. (This service is more common in the West. Eastern dog lovers, maybe here's a business opportunity for you!) |
| | Dog Walking/ Pet Sitting  Poop-Removal Service  Dog Grooming | Service providers who come to your home, including dog walkers, pet sitters, poop removers, and some groomers, are found under the heading **All Neighborhoods** in the listings. Call to confirm the service areas. |
| | Low-Cost Vaccination Clinics | Vaccination clinics at pet superstores are usually offered on a monthly basis. |
| | On-Site Pet Adoptions | Each section lists stores and other businesses that hold adoptions (usually on a monthly basis.) Also see Puppy Starter Kit, p.183 for other resources. |
| | Shuttle Service | Businesses that offer shuttle service (in the listings as **(S)**) may only offer it to and from business or, as in the case of many pet sitters, offer rides around town. |

# Philadelphia Proper

## ALTERNATIVE PRODUCTS/SERVICES

**All Neighborhoods**
All Paws Pet Sitting

**Bella Vista/Queen Village**
Queen Village Dog & Cat Grooming

## ANESTHESIA-FREE TEETH CLEANING

**Bella Vista/Queen Village**
Oh So Pretty
Queen Village Dog & Cat Grooming

## ANIMAL HOSPITALS & VET CLINICS

**Rhawnhurst**
Rhawnhurst Animal Hospital

**West Philly**
O'Neal Animal Hospital

## CAT SERVICES/PRODUCTS AVAILABLE

**Bella Vista/Queen Village**
Accent on Animals
Poochie Styles

**Center City**
The Barking Lot
Bonejour Pet Supply

**Juniata**
PetSmart: Juniata

**Manayunk**
Furlong's Pet Store
Petco: City Line Ave

**Northeast Philly**
Petco: Northeast Philly
PetSmart: Northeast Philly

**Port Richmond**
Petco: Aramingo Ave.

**Rhawnhurst**
PetSmart: Cottman

**South Philly**
Petco: South Philly

# CITY DOG PICKS

**Philadelphia**
Fairmount Park
PhilaPets

**Bella Vista**
Chic Petique, The

**Center City**
Canine Cottage Dog Grooming

**Northern Liberties**
See Spot Stay **(S)**

**Rittenhouse Square**
Rittenhouse Square Pet Supplies

**South Philly**
Philadelphia K-9 Academy

**Wynnefield**
Beverly's Dog Shop

# DOG BOARDING

**Cedarbrook**
Dog Salon, The

**Northeast Philly**
Doggie World Daycare, Inc.

**Northern Liberties**
Rainbow Grooming Spa
See Spot Stay **(S)**

**Roxborough**
AAA Country Boarding and Doggie Daycare

**West Philly**
O'Neal Animal Hospital

**Wynnefield**
Beverly's Dog Shop

# DOG DAY CARE

**Northeast Philly**
Doggie World Daycare, Inc.

**Northern Liberties**
See Spot Stay **(S)**

**Roxborough**
AAA Country Boarding and Doggie Daycare

# DOG GROOMING

**Bella Vista/Queen Village**
Oh So Pretty
Poochie Styles
Queen Village Dog and Cat Grooming

**Cedarbrook**
Dog Salon, The

**Center City**
Barking Lot, The
Canine Cottage Dog Grooming

**Germantown**
Groomin' Room, The

**Juniata**
PetSmart: Juniata

**Manayunk**
Canine Clippers

**Northeast Philly**
Bobbie Lyn Canine Grooming
Doggie World Daycare, Inc.
Petco: Northeast Philly
PetSmart: Northeast Philly

**Northern Liberties**
Rainbow Grooming Spa

**Port Richmond**
Petco: Aramingo Ave

**Rhawnhurst**
Dog Zone, The
PetSmart Cottman

**Roxborough**
Clippendales

**South Philly**
Petco: South Philly

**Wynnefield**
Beverly's Dog Shop

## DOG PARKS & TRAILS

**Philadelphia**
Fairmount Park

**Chestnut Hill**
Pastorius Park

**Fairmount**
Eastern State Dog Pen

**Germantown**
Carpenter Woods Dog Park

**Northeast Philly**
Liberty Lands Park

## DOG TRAINING

**All Neighborhoods**
K-9 Training & Behavioral Therapy
Proper Paws

**Juniata**
PetSmart: Juniata

**Northeast Philly**
Doggie World Daycare, Inc.
PetSmart: Northeast Philly

**Rhawnhurst**
PetSmart: Cottman

**South Philly**
Philadelphia K-9 Academy
Petco: South Philly

## DOG TRAINING

**All Neighborhoods**
K-9 Training & Behavioral Therapy
Proper Paws

**Juniata**
PetSmart: Juniata

**Northeast Philly**
Doggie World Daycare, Inc.
PetSmart: Northeast Philly

**Rhawnhurst**
PetSmart: Cottman

**South Philly**
Philadelphia K-9 Academy
Petco: South Philly

## DOG WALKING/PET SITTING

**All Neighborhoods**

All Paws Pet Sitting
La Dolce Vita Pet Care **(S)**
Pampered Pets
PhiladelphiaPawsandClaws.com **(S)**
PhilaPets
UC Pet Tenders

## DOG-CENTRIC RESOURCES

Schuylkill River Park Dog Owners Association

## LOW-COST VACCINATION CLINICS

**Manayunk**
Petco: City Line Ave

**Northeast Philly**
Petco: Northeast

**Port Richmond**
Petco: Aramingo Ave

**South Philly**
Petco: South Philly

## ON-SITE PET ADOPTIONS

**Juniata**
PetSmart: Juniata

**Manayunk**
Petco: City Line Ave

**Northeast Philly**
Petco: Northeast Philly
PetSmart: Northeast Philly

**Rhawnhurst**
PetSmart: Cottman

**South Philly**
Petco: South Philly

## PET-SUPPLY STORES

**Bella Vista/Queen Village**
Accent on Animals: Philadelphia
Chic Petique, The
Queen Village Dog & Cat Grooming

**Center City**
Bonejour Pet Supply

**Chestnut Hill**
Bone Appetite, The: Chestnut Hill
Chestnut Hill Dog Bakery

**Juniata**
PetSmart: Juniata

**Manayunk**
Furlong's Pet Store
Petco: City Line Ave

**Northeast Philly**
Bobbie Lyn Canine Grooming
Petco: Northeast Philly
PetSmart: Northeast Philly

**Port Richmond**
Petco: Aramingo Ave

**Rhawnhurst**
PetSmart: Cottman

**Rittenhouse Square**
Rittenhouse Square Pet Supplies

**South Philly**
Petco: South Philly

# PHOTOGRAPHY/PAINTINGS

**Northeast Philly**
Petco: Northeast Philadelphia

# SELF-SERVE DOG GROOMING

**Northeast Philly**
Petco: Northeast Philly

**Rhawnhurst**
Dog Zone, The

# SHUTTLE SERVICE

**All Neighborhoods**
La Dolce Vita Dog Care
Pampered Pets

**Northern Liberties**
See Spot Stay

# General Listings

## AAA Country Boarding and Doggie Daycare

(215) 483-2873
8835 Ridge Ave
(E of Manatawna Ave)
Philadelphia, PA 19128
**Hours:** By Appt
**Payment:** Checks
**Price Range:** $$

This horse farm-cum-boarding facility is a puppy paradise. Conveniently located at the edge of Philadelphia and Montgomery counties, AAA is in the capable hands of married couple Ralph and Kim, who live in the farmhouse. All dogs are matched with playmates of similar temperament. Then, they're set free on fenced fields thick with pasture grass. At night, they're tucked to sleep in their own kennels. Rates start at $15/ night for smaller dogs, $45/night for larger dogs. Basic beds are provided or you can bring your own. Administering medication is considered a standard part of the service. They fill up fast during the holidays and summertime so plan ahead.

## Accent on Animals: Philadelphia

(215) 625-8420
804 South St
(@ 8th St)
Philadelphia, PA 19147
**Hours:** Mon – Sat 10 AM – 6 PM
Sun 11 AM – 5 PM
**Payment:** Credit Cards
**Price Range:** $$

Think twice before bringing your dog along to this store, as the narrow aisles afford just enough room for one person to peruse the shelves. But what they lack in space, they make up for with scads of goods. Accent on Animals offers everything from commercial-brand dry and canned foods, toys and dog beds to a great selection of shampoos and vitamins. People offerings include stationery and breed-specific T-shirts. The friendly and helpful staff are obvious "animal people." If you're going to the Philadelphia location, bring change for the meters.

## All Paws Pet Sitting
(267) 252-8488
**Hours:** By Appt
**Payment:** Checks
**Price Range:** $$

What makes this pet sitter unique is his 20-minute pet massages ($20 per session). Mike is a licensed massage therapist, who will happily demonstrate his technique so you can work out your dog's knots yourself. As for his pet-sitting services, a standard visit includes a 30-minute walk ($15). If you schedule All Paws at least five times a week, you pay only $12 a visit. He'll collect your mail and bring in the garbage cans, but Mike doesn't do vacation care. Serving all of Philadelphia.

## Barking Lot, The
(215) 238-1017
244 S 11th St
(@ Locust St)
Philadelphia, PA 19107
**Hours:** Mon 9 AM – 5:30 PM
Tue – Thu 9 AM – 5 PM
Fri 9 AM – 7 PM
**Payment:** Checks
**Price Range:** $$$

Owner Karen's expertise is — pay attention here — aggressive dogs, although mild-mannered pooches are, of course, also welcome. So are cats. She's even untangled rabbit and hamster fur. Standard grooming starts at around $50 for a medium-sized dog, but as anyone who's ever had their chow trimmed down to pomeranian stature knows, a few extra bucks are a small price to pay for a good cut. Small animals are always hand dried with towels. Big dogs are cage-dried with temperature-controlled cage dryers and two large fans. A few days' advance booking is usually fine; allow a week during the holiday season. The one drawback: The Barking Lot has no parking lot.

## Beverly's Dog Shop

(215) 477-5599
Duffield House
3701 Conshohocken Ave
(@ E Country Club Rd)
Philadelphia, PA 19131
**Hours:** Tue – Sat 9 AM – 3 PM
**Payment:** Checks
**Price Range:** $$

Owner Beverly covers her studio walls with pictures of
champion dogs, complete with trophy, in their moment of glory
— perhaps as inspiration. She is serious about creating the per-
fect cut in her small, upbeat salon. Dogs are washed with Crazy
Dog brand shampoo in varying scents (oatmeal and aloe vera
also available). She starts the drying process with a temperature-
controlled cage dryer (under supervision), and then finishes
drying by hand before hand scissoring them for a smooth, even
cut. Cuts start at $40. If your pup's got dreads — de-matting
long-haired dogs (starting at $50) is a house specialty. Beverly
also provides in-home boarding for established customers. Call
two weeks in advance to schedule an appointment.

## Bobbie Lyn Canine Grooming

(215) 677-3784
2200 Michener St #5
(@ Evans St)
Philadelphia, PA 19115
**Hours:** Mon – Thu 9 AM – 7 PM
**Payment:** Cash
**Price Range:** $$

Two groomers wield the blades at Bobbie Lyn Canine
Grooming. The groomers use razors and clippers for cuts.
Grooming, starting at $35 for a medium-sized dog, includes
a bath, cut, nail clipping, and ear cleaning. And all dogs are
hand dried. The salon cannot accommodate extra-large and
particularly time-consuming breeds, like sheepdogs over 125
pounds. Appointments should be made about a week in
advance, although walk-ins can sometimes be squeezed in.
Around holidays, the shop is busier, so two to three weeks
advance notice is recommended. An assortment of pet
supplies, including treats and collars, is available at the
front of the store.

# Bone Appetite, The: Chestnut Hill

(215) 247-4292
8505 Germantown Ave
(@ W Highland Ave)
Philadelphia, PA 19118
www.theboneappetite.com
**Hours:** Mon – Thu 10 AM – 5:30 PM, Fri 10 AM – 6 PM
Sat 9:30 AM – 5 PM, Sun 12 PM – 4 PM
**Payment:** Credit Cards
**Price Range:** $$$

This chic doggie bakery offers two locations: one right on the Main Line, proudly perched among some of the area's smartest retail space, and another in historic Chestnut Hill. Despite its swank company and polished appearance, the friendly staff is down to earth and eager to pamper your pet with generous free samples. Offerings include homemade bakery treats, birthday cakes, custom collars, painted bowls (complete with your pup's paw print), and pet beds in your choice of fabrics. Imagine lots of pick-me-ups for impromptu gift giving, and you start to feel Bone Appetite's fun, fresh-baked appeal.

# Bonejour Pet Supply

(215) 574-1225
14 N 3rd St
(between Market & Arch Sts)
Philadelphia, PA 19106
www.bonejourpetsupply.com
**Hours:** Mon – Fri 11 AM – 7 PM
Sat 11 AM – 5 PM, Sun 12 PM – 4 PM
**Payment:** Credit Cards, Checks
**Price Range:** $$$

This small shop's owner, Julie, is big on customer service. Bonejour's Web site proclaims their philosophy: Every dog's a rock star. Julie stocks the stuff that will keep your doggish diva in perfect pitch — treats like Liberty Bell cookies ($9 a bag) and fresh dog-sized Philly cheese-steak treats ($4 for one) and upscale dog foods. The store has everything from pricey furniture like the velvet chaise and chair ($120 – $130), in zebra- and leopard-print, respectively, to matching faux-leather jackets for person and pet, as well as fleecy totes. Julie even offers delivery service for just a few bucks.

## Canine Clippers

(215) 482-9091
4345-47 Cresson St
(E of Grape St)
Philadelphia, PA 19127
**Hours:** Tue – Sat 8 AM – 4 PM
**Payment:** Checks
**Price Range:** $$

In the reception area of this salon, you are greeted by a mural of "Dog Rushmore," starring owner/groomer Jim's two dogs Micky and Minnie as well as Candy and Cindy, a good friends' pups. Jim's specialty is hand plucking soft-coated Wheaton terriers. He is also adept at breed-standard cuts for other breeds. Dogs are hand dried with forced-air dryers. Two bathers assist in getting dogs in and out in a timely manner. Cuts start at around $30. A day's notice is okay for a bath, but plan a week ahead for full grooming.

## Canine Cottage Dog Grooming

(215) 331-6300
6301 Cottage St
(@ Robbins St)
Philadelphia, PA 19135
www.caninecottage.net
**Hours:** Mon – Sat 9 AM – 5 PM
**Payment:** Credit Cards
**Price Range:** $$$

With groomers boasting 30 years of experience, your dog is sure to leave Canine Cottage looking fabulous. This full-service grooming salon offers several options: There's the full groom ($50 & up), which includes a thorough brush, trim, ear cleaning, nail clipping, bath and fluff dry. Popular add-on treatments include the medicated hot-oil bath ($50 & up), in which your dog is placed in a rich oatmeal-shampoo bath and then massaged with hot oil. And for owners on the run, there's the bath and go ($10 – $40), but since your dog leaves the salon damp, it's probably best to skip this service except in the warmer months.

## Carpenter Woods Dog Park
(215) 683-0200
Wissahickon Ave & Mt. Pleasant Ave
(@ Greene St & Sedgwick St)
Philadelphia, PA 19119
**Hours:** Every Day: Sunrise to Sunset
**Payment:** Free
Domesticated and wild animals abound at this peaceful glen in Philadelphia's Mount Airy district. Bird watchers say it's one of the best places in the Delaware Valley to see migrating warblers — it's also one of the best spots to see pups and people communing with nature. Somehow the warblers and woofers have struck a delicate balance here and residents would like to keep it that way. So remember: keep your pet on a leash. A sunset walk through the park's lush sylvan landscape and expansive trail system is enough to make anyone . . . well, warble.

## Chestnut Hill Dog Bakery
(215) 242-4408
8229 Germantown Ave
(@ Southampton Ave)
Philadelphia, PA 19118
**Hours:** Thu – Fri 9 AM – 5 PM
       Sat – Sun 8 AM – 5 PM
**Payment:** Credit Cards
**Price Range:** $
This modest booth nestled inside the granola-chic Chestnut Hill Farmers Market features low-fat, preservative-free dog treats designed to not add bulk or clog the arteries. The treats have a shelf life of about two months, but loyal customers pop in at least every few weeks to cruise the bins for a half-pound's worth of snacks. This side business operated by dog owner and insurance representative Tom Monahan can get crowded on weekends; repeat customers know to stop by on Thursdays or Fridays if they want fast-selling flavors (apple-cinnamon is a favorite).

## Chic Petique, The

(215) 629-1733
616 S 3rd St
(between Bainbridge & South Sts)
Philadelphia, PA 19147
**Hours:** Mon – Sat 10 AM – 8 PM
　　　　Sun 10 AM – 6 PM
**Payment:** Credit Cards
**Price Range:** $$$

Just around the corner from South Street, Chic Petique is hip without hauteur. This retail wonderland bridges the gap between tasty and healthy dog foods. You can tempt your dog with gourmet treats that look like sushi trays or browse through the racks of tuxedos and evening gowns for the delicate set. The shelves blaze with pup-centric personality, expressed in fancy dishes, fleece beds, and toys — including menorah-shaped plushes and politician squeakers. But owner Lindsay is more into the pups than the props — she also runs a nonprofit canine rescue.

## Clippendales

(215) 482-4840
6208 Ridge Ave
(W of Leverington Ave)
Philadelphia, PA 19128
**Hours:** Tue – Fri 8 AM – 5 PM
　　　　Sat 8 AM – 1 PM
**Payment:** Checks
**Price Range:** $$

Dogs form a welcoming committee behind the counter as you enter this bright and spacious grooming salon. Owner/groomer Susan prefers a cage-free environment where dogs are treated with love, hugs, and kisses rather than tranquilizers. Dogs are hand-scissored and hand-dried. Grooming, starting at $50 for a medium-sized dog, is by appointment only, and scheduling usually requires leaving a message and waiting for Susan to return your call. A few days' notice is usually sufficient.

## Dog Salon, The

(215) 569-2555
1123 Ivy Hill Rd
(between Cheltenham & Stenton Aves)
Philadelphia, PA 19150
**Hours:** Mon – Thu 8 AM – 2 PM, Fri 8 AM – 5 PM
Sat 8 AM – 11 AM
**Payment:** Credit Cards
**Price Range:** $$

This grooming salon-cum-boarding facility is a Philly institution. With 20 years' experience each, the two groomers are more than capable of handling any breed that walks through the door, delivering both breed-standard cuts as well as casual clips. Dogs are dried with warm-air dryers both by hand and in cages. Boarded dogs are housed in climate-controlled kennels that connect to outdoor runs. The boarding facility is open seven days a week, though pickups or drop-offs outside the restrictive regular hours must be made by appointment. Book appointments at least a week in advance.

## Dog Zone, The

(215) 722-2278
7700 Castor Ave
(@ Lansing St)
Philadelphia, PA 19152
**Hours:** Mon – Fri 8 AM – 5 PM
Sat 9 AM – 5 PM
**Payment:** Credit Cards, Checks
**Price Range:** $$

There's nothing like a visit to the groomer to transform a shaggy dog into a well-coiffed canine. All breeds, big and small, are welcome for beautification at the Dog Zone. Skilled scissoristas can handle breed-specific cuts as well as casual clips and brushouts. Once they've been groomed, dogs get to hang out in a big, cage-free, indoor/outdoor play space until they get picked up. If you're looking for less than the works, you can wash your own dog for $12. Dog Zone is committed to keeping customers happy and offers a written satisfaction-guarantee on all of their services.

## Doggie World Daycare, Inc.
(215) 238-7200
858-62 N 3rd St
(between Brown & Poplar Sts)
Philadelphia, PA 19123
www.doggieworld.net
**Hours:** Mon – Fri 7 AM – 7 PM
        Sat 9 AM – 6 PM, Sun 4 PM – 7 PM
**Payment:** Credit Cards
**Price Range:** $$
A fenced-in pup playground with plenty of equipment,
supervised indoor play rooms, and a leisure den with TV and
VCR all but guarantee your pup will find his place at Doggie
World. Staff promises that "proper training habits will be rein-
forced." Daily day-care rates range from $19 to $27; overnights
range from $29 to $39. Other services include full-service
grooming and lessons by APDT-certified trainer Karen DeBoer
Privitello, who teaches obedience and agility. Check out the
Web site — the online photo gallery gives you a great feel for
the facility.

## Eastern State Dog Pen
Brown St & Corinthian Ave
(@ 22nd St)
Philadelphia, PA 19130
www.fairmountdog.org
**Hours:** Every Day: Sunrise to Sunset
**Payment:** Free
Despite its name, and its location behind what used to be a
penitentiary, this is not a prison for pups. At one time nothing
more than an undesirable patch of land, this doggie hangout
has undergone a much welcomed makeover. Eastern State is
now replete with miles of protective fence, fresh stone, and
lush green grass. The Pen bustles steadily from dawn until
dusk, and summertime is especially busy with off-leash yappy
hours and barbecues. Plenty of cold water bottles and
sunblock are recommended for summertime, as trees are not
part of the renewed landscape.

## Fairmount Park

(215) 685-0000
4231 N Concourse Dr
(@ E Memorial Hall Dr)
Philadelphia, PA 19131
www.fairmountpark.org/
**Hours:** Every Day: Sunrise to Sunset
**Payment:** Free

Fairmount Park — all 9,200 acres of it — is comprised of
Philadelphia's 62 neighborhood parks. Needless to say, it's
quite popular with dogs all over town. Many people take
their pups to the curiously named Forbidden Drive (don't
let the name scare you), a wide gravel trail on the west side
of Wissahickon Creek, located off Lincoln Drive below
Wissahickon Avenue. On Wissahickon's east side, you'll find
rugged trails and steep slopes for challenge seekers. Leash-free
activities can be had at the very popular dog run, located on
25th Street between Pine and Locust. The run offers separate
areas for big and small dogs, comfy benches, a water fountain,
and lighting for evening strolls.

## Furlong's Pet Store

(215) 508-2508
4223 Main St
(between Lock & Station Sts)
Philadelphia, PA 19127
**Hours:** Mon – Sun 11 AM – 7 PM
**Payment:** Credit Cards
**Price Range:** $$

Located on Main Street in the heart of Manayunk's shopping
district, this small store has plenty to offer adventure lovers.
Active, outdoorsy dogs and their owners will enjoy the superb
selection of camping tents, life vests, first-aid kits, sunscreen,
goggles, and backpacks. They also sell herbal dog shampoos,
seat belts, leashes (training and stretchable), breed-specific
leash hooks, dishes, toys, and cleanup baggies and products.
Dogs are welcome so long as they're on leash. You can also
order from their Web site — most products ship the same day.

## Groomin' Room, The

(215) 624-7666
7540 Frankford Ave
Philadelphia, PA 19136
www.thegroominroom.com
**Hours:** Mon 8 AM – 2 PM, Tue – Thu 8 AM – 6 PM
Fri 8 AM – 2 PM, Sat 8 AM – 4 PM
**Payment:** Credit Cards, Checks
**Price Range:** $$
At the Groomin' Room, experienced hand-scissoring experts can handle any cut you desire for your dog. Full grooming services include a massaging bath, ear cleaning, nail trimming, pad shaving, cologne application, and a bow or bandanna. Other offerings include the FURminator shedless treatment — that can reduce shedding up to 80 percent, as well as teeth brushing and baths with specialty shampoos (try the Golden Almond). Dogs are fluff dried by hand, with warm-air dryers. Prices start at $40 for a medium-sized dog. Metered parking is available on the street in front of the shop.

## K-9 Training & Behavioral Therapy

(215) 551-5254
Philadelphia, PA
www.k-9training.org
**Hours:** By Appt
**Payment:** Checks
**Price Range:** $$
Word of mouth and local television appearances have garnered Pat Bentz, a dog trainer since 1978, a truly standout reputation. Using verbal communication as well as hand signals combined with "life rewards," such as treats, toys, and attention, she customizes lessons to fit the needs of you and your dog. She'll even leave you with handouts for practice. Pat offers one- and two-hour behavior consultations (one hour/$70; two hours/$150) as well as four- and seven-week private-training programs. Her areas of expertise include teaching your dog to co-exist with a new baby or an old cat, and to stop attacking visitors. K-9's pre- and post-adoption support and puppy training are also in demand.

## La Dolce Vita Pet Care

(267) 242-5190
P.O. Box 63765
Philadelphia, PA 19147
http://ladolcevitapetcare.blogspot.com
**Hours:** By Appt
**Payment:** Checks
**Price Range:** $$

The dog's life doesn't get much better than La Dolce Vita. This full-service pet-care business, owned and operated by Jessica Dolce, pulls out all the stops. Dolce offers pet sitting and dog walking (a 30-minute visit runs $15; an hour is $25) and pet-taxi and pet-food-delivery services. They'll also bring in the mail, adjust the shades, and turn lights on and off to give your home a lived-in look while you're away. Jessica and her team of sitters also get points for their volunteer work with Alliance for Animals, making the good life possible for the area's orphaned animals. Serving Pennsport, Bella Vista, Queen Village, Italian Market, and Society Hill.

## Liberty Lands Park

(215) 627-6562
913-961 North 3rd St
(@ Poplar St)
Philadelphia, PA 19123
**Hours:** Every Day: Sunrise to Sunset
**Payment:** Free

This rehabbed two-acre green space is a communal meeting spot for dog owners, gardeners, families, and artists, who flock here on a daily basis to this slowly gentrifying, industrial North Philadelphia neighborhood. A well-placed fence, installed by the Northern Liberties Neighborhood Association, has improved relations between the dog and gardening communities. Off-leash romping is frowned upon, but most will look the other way so long as overzealous pups are kept at a respectable distance from playing children. Keep an eye out for the occasional stray piece of glass among the patchy grass in the park's large, sun-drenched center square.

## Oh So Pretty

(267) 767-7532
614 S 3rd St
(@ Bainbridge St)
Philadelphia, PA 19147
**Hours:** Tue – Sat 9 AM – 5 PM
**Payment:** Credit Cards
**Price Range:** $$

Pictures of happy dogs lining the walls create a welcoming atmosphere at Oh So Pretty. Boasting over a decade of experience, owner Tina Grello is happy to take the time to talk to you about your vision of your pup's cut. She can handle both breed-specific and pet cuts — using hand scissors or clippers. Grooming starts at $40 – $45 for a medium-sized dog. All dogs are dried by hand. Stinky breath can be remedied with on-site teeth cleaning. Book at least four or five days in advance. They are usually unable to accommodate last-minute appointments and walk-ins. Parking outside may be difficult; try Bainbridge one block south of South Street.

## O'Neal Animal Hospital

(215) 386-3293
4424 Market St
(between 44th & 45th Sts)
Philadelphia, PA 19104
**Hours:** Mon – Fri 9 AM – 5 PM
**Payment:** Credit Cards, Checks
**Price Range:** $

Pets and their owners crowd the waiting room at this West Philly hospital. The resident vet, David Littlejohn, DVM, who spends a fair amount of time with each four-legged patient before making any diagnosis, is about as far from an "on-to-the-next"-type vet as you can get. A routine exam costs a very reasonable $29. The hospital is equipped for surgeries and also offers boarding. For $15 a night, your dog will reside in one of the seven 4 x 7 runs, and will be fed and watered, but not walked.

## Pampered Pets
(215) 849-6960
Philadelphia, PA
**Hours:** By Appt
**Payment:** Checks
**Price Range:** $$
The Best of Care When You're Not There! is owner Judy Lloyd's motto for her pet-sitting, dog-walking, and pet-taxi business. Owners are asked to complete a Pampered Pets Personal Care Form, which asks for information such as your pet's favorite word or phrase. Filling ice cubes in the water bowl on a hot day, or changing the channel so your dog can enjoy his favorite program on TV come standard. Pampered Pets leaves a report card, complete with notes on your dog's day, at the end of each visit. Serving dogs and other housebound pets primarily in Chestnut Hill and Mt. Airy.

## Pastorius Park
(215) 247-6696
Hartwell Ln @ Millman St
Philadelphia, PA  19118
www.chestnuthillpa.com/pastorius.asp
**Hours:** Every Day: Dawn to Dusk
**Payment:** Free
Boasting several acres and a pond, this fabulous park is located smack in the middle of Chestnut Hill. Technically, this is not an off-leash dog park. However, at any given time there are usually at least a few dogs running free. During the summer months, there are open-air concerts every Wednesday night, so parking is tough and letting your dog run free may be frowned upon. Neighborhood residents aren't exactly thrilled with the recent influx of canines, so if you do visit, be vigilant about poop clean-up and make sure your pup is under your control at all times. Also, keep in mind that this is also a play area for neighborhood children.

# Petco

www.petco.com
**Payment:** Credit Cards, Checks
**Price Range:** $/$$/$$$

## Petco: Aramingo Ave

(215) 423-4414
3300 Aramingo Ave
(@ E Westmoreland St)
Philadelphia, PA 19134
**Hours:** Mon – Sat 9 AM – 10 PM
Sun 10 AM – 8 PM

## Petco: City Line Ave

(215) 878-3203
4508 City Line Ave
(between Belmont Ave & Rte 23)
Philadelphia, PA 19131
**Hours:** Mon – Sat 9 AM – 9 PM
Sun 10 AM – 7 PM

## Petco: Northeast Philly

(215) 671-9601
9717 Roosevelt Blvd
between Bowler & Lott Sts
Philadelphia, PA 19114
**Hours:** Mon – Sat 9 AM – 10 PM
Sun 9 AM – 8 PM

## Petco: South Philly

(215) 462-2080
2360 W Oregon Ave
(between 22nd & 24th Sts)
Philadelphia, PA 19145
**Hours:** Mon – Sat 9 AM – 9 PM
Sun 10 AM – 6 PM
**Price Range:** $$

For one-stop shopping it's hard to beat the convenience and value of this superstore with locations all over the country. Petco makes it their mission to provide customers with the food, supplements and products they want for their animals. Their bed selection runs the gamut, from orthopedic mattresses, along with sheets and throws, to chaises that would do an interior decorator proud. Get a P.A.L.S. (Petco Animal Lovers Save) card to take advantage of discounts; you may also want to check out their Top Dog program, which offers even greater saving to their most loyal customers. Check the listing for each store's hours and specific service offerings.

## PetSmart

www.petsmart.com
**Payment:** Credit Cards, Checks
**Price Range:** $/$$/$$$

## PetSmart: Cottman

(215) 728-7166
7501 Horracks St
(@ Shelmire Ave)
Philadelphia, PA 19152
**Hours:** Mon – Sat 9 AM – 9 PM
Sun 10 AM – 6 PM

## PetSmart: Northeast Philly

(215) 698-8320
11000 Roosevelt Blvd
(between Haldeman Ave & Bennett Dr)
Philadelphia, PA 19116
**Hours:** Mon – Sat 9 AM – 9 PM
Sun 10 AM – 6 PM

## PetSmart: Juniata

(215) 743-9602
4640-60 E Roosevelt Blvd
(between Adams Ave & Langdon St)
Philadelphia, PA 19124
**Hours:** Mon – Sat 9 AM – 9 PM
Sun 10 AM – 6 PM

This standout superstore is to pet owners what Home Depot is to homeowners. PetSmart stocks an unbelievably wide range of products that will meet almost any budget. They carry the better dog food brands — including Bil-Jac. And whenever possible, they offer all-natural options in their selection of treats, supplements and skin products. A viewing window allows see-for-yourself grooming so you don't have to worry about what happens behind closed doors. They get major points for promoting their adoptions all the time. And they have a staff that's always available to advise you and to help you find what you need. It's places like PetSmart that give superstores a good name. Check the listing for each store's hours and specific service offerings.

## Philadelphia K-9 Academy

(215) 221-1197
3900 N 2nd St
between Luzerne St & Erie Ave
Philadelphia, PA 19140
**Hours:** Call for a schedule
**Payment:** Checks
**Price Range:** $$$

Frank and Edna run this no-nonsense training facility that turns wayward pups into obedient angels. To be admitted, you and your pup must pass their free entrance test. Don't worry, unless you're the type that's looking to train your pit bull to attack, you shouldn't have a problem. Positive reinforcement is their preferred training method — but they don't believe in food rewards. For $400, you'll get 10 one-hour semi-private classes (three-dog max). And if you run into problems down the road — say you move in a couple of years and your dog is marking all over your new place — Philadelphia K-9 will help you resolve those issues too. Past clients consider Frank and Edna part of the family.

## PhiladelphiaPawsandClaws.com

(215) 482-6799
http://philadelphiapets2.homestead.com/files/index.html
**Hours:** Mon – Sun 6:30 AM – 11:30 PM
**Payment:** Credit Cards
**Price Range:** $$

With a staff of five pet sitters and an 11-year track record, PhiladelphiaPawsandClaws.com (yes, that is their actual name) operates like a well-oiled machine. And judging by their 14-page customer guide, which outlines their policies, including a free consultation and trial walk as well as a no-service policy for certain breeds, PawsandClaws is nothing if not attentive to detail. Treats provided by the company are a nice bonus to the $15 walk. Two to three weeks notice is best for vacation requests, but if you're looking for holiday care, make arrangements two to four months in advance. Bartering home-improvement services, time-shares, or landscaping for pet care isn't out of the question.

## PhilaPets

(215) 893-0894
Philadelphia, PA
www.philapets.com
**Hours:** Mon – Sun 7 AM – 9 PM
**Payment:** Checks
**Price Range:** $$

PhilaPets has an impressive 16-member staff which includes
several veterinary students and certified veterinary technicians.
At $15, walks last from 25 to 45 minutes, and sitters also
spend some time just hanging out with your dog in your home,
making visits last up to an hour. And if your dog doesn't mind
playing with others, they offer longer group walks. The user-
friendly Web site allows clients to book and cancel pet servic-
es and see which sitter will be walking their dog. Surcharges
include a $5 holiday premium as well as a $3 charge for
administering meds, plus a meds tutorial fee of $15.

## Poochie Styles

(215) 545-4699
1302 South St
(@ 13th St)
Philadelphia, PA  19147
**Hours:** Tue – Sat 8:30 AM – 4:30 PM
**Payment:** Credit Cards
**Price Range:** $

Friendly service, custom cuts, and affordable prices (starting
at $30) are what make Poochie Styles so popular. This small,
clean grooming facility is owned and operated by Tiffany
Glover — a certified master groomer from the New York
School of Dog Grooming. Poochie Styles offers anesthesia-
free teeth cleaning in addition to grooming services. Shampoo
options include the heavenly smelling Crazy Dog, as well as
Fresh & Clean and oatmeal. Dogs are cage dried under
supervision. If you cannot pick up your dog immediately,
the groomer can babysit him for a few hours. Walk-ins are
welcome, space permitting, but appointments are
recommended.

## Proper Paws

(215) 463-3813
www.properpaws.com
**Hours:** Mon – Fri 12 PM – 7 PM
Sat 10 AM – 5 PM
**Payment:** Credit Cards
**Price Range:** $$

Founded in 2000, Proper Paws makes its bones on private dog training. All trainers are certified by the American Pet Dog Trainers Association and are approved by the AKC as Canine Good Citizen evaluators. Lessons, conducted in your home, are tailored to suit the needs of you and your dog. Classes cover a range of topics, including puppy training basics, behavior modification (including aggression and separation anxiety) and advanced obedience training. Sessions run between 30 and 60 minutes. Each individual lesson costs $65, with discounts for multiple sessions. A phone consultation is required prior to beginning any training program.

## Queen Village Dog & Cat Grooming

(215) 925-1499
745 South 2nd St
(@ Fitzwater St)
Philadelphia, PA 19147
**Hours:** Mon – Sat 9 AM – 5 PM
**Payment:** Cash
**Price Range:** $$

In business 33 years, this pet salon keeps clients happy by consistently delivering efficient, affordable service. They only offer pet cuts, complete with a supervised cage dry — and can get your pup out the door in about an hour. Aromatherapy and hypoallergenic products are available upon request. Nervous owners are invited to watch the grooming process from start to finish. There is a small selection of pet supplies — mostly toys and impulse items — to browse through while you wait. Schedule appointments four to five days in advance. Cats welcome.

## Rainbow Grooming Spa

(215) 634-4884
1746 N Howard St
(@ Palmer St)
Philadelphia, PA 19122
**Hours:** Mon – Sat 8:30 AM – 6 PM
Closing time is flexible depending on appointments.
**Payment:** Cash
**Price Range:** $$

The casual atmosphere belies this salon's quality cuts and grooming. Offerings include hand scissoring (starting at $35 for a medium sized-dog), hand-stripping ($10 – 20 as an add-on service), carting, clipping, brush-outs and FURminator de-shedding treatments. The drying process never involves hot air, but rather forced-air drying without a nozzle, cage drying with fans (under close supervision), or a hair dryer set on cool for smaller dogs. All breeds are welcome and boarding, starting at $12 per night, is also available. A couple of days notice for appointments is recommended, but walk-ins are not unheard of.

## Rhawnhurst Animal Hospital

(215) 333-8888
7905 Bustleton Ave
(@ Borbeck Ave)
Philadelphia, PA 19152
**Hours:** Mon – Tue 9 AM – 7 PM, Wed 9 AM – 4 PM
Thu – Fri 9 AM – 7 PM, Sat 9 AM – 11:30 PM
**Payment:** Credit Cards, Checks
**Price Range:** $

This clean, spacious animal hospital is friendly, through and through, from the receptionists to the vet techs, to the vets — all are people-pleasing animal lovers. A standard checkup for your dog will run you $36, but you're not just paying for a poking and prodding; the veterinarians aim to educate you as well. There is no grooming or boarding at this facility. However, Rhawnhurst is affiliated with the Elkins Park Veterinary Hospital (some of the vets practice there as well), which has its own boarding kennels.

## Rittenhouse Square Pet Supplies

(215) 569-2555
135 S 20th St
(@ Moravian St)
Philadelphia, PA 19103
**Hours:** Mon – Fri 10 AM – 7 PM
　　　　Sat 11 AM – 5 PM
**Payment:** Credit Cards
**Price Range:** $$

Parking can be a challenge on this popular block of shops, but
it's worth the effort. Treats abound in this quaint boutique that
is jam-packed with toys, beds, collars, dishes, grooming sup-
plies, and pet clothing. Dog food options includes brands like
Science Diet, Nutro, Wellness, Nova, and Breeder's Choice.
Be sure to check out the hot sellers — hand-knit dog sweaters,
selling for $25 to $40.

## Schuylkill River Park Dog Owners' Association

P.O. Box 30246
Philadelphia, PA 19103
www.phillyfido.net
**Hours:** Meetings twice a year
**Payment:** Checks
**Price Range:** $

Originally formed in 2002 to raise money to resurface and
maintain the dog run at Fairmount Park, Schuylkill River Park
Dog Owners Association is now 150 members strong.
It contributes to the community in all sorts of ways: for exam-
ple, assisting a young bite victim in getting vaccination records
for the dog that bit her, so she wouldn't need to undergo
rabies shots. Members own all different types of dogs, and
hail from New Jersey, Wynnewood, South Philadelphia, and
Germantown. Formal meetings take place twice yearly, though
many members meet informally at other times — often at the
dog park. This organization is a great community resource for
animal lovers. Check the Web site for upcoming events.

## See Spot Stay

(215) 769-3313
685 North Broad St
(@ Melon St)
Philadelphia, PA 19123
www.seespotstay.com
**Hours:** Mon – Fri 7 AM – 7 PM
Sat 9 AM – 5 PM
**Payment:** Credit Cards, Checks
**Price Range:** $$

Day-care dogs are grouped by size, temperament, and age, with an eight-dog limit and a staff member supervising each group. Groups are rotated outside several times a day, with a two-hour rest period in the middle of the day. The facility boasts four playrooms and two lounge rooms, complete with couches and beds, and kiddie pools outdoors in the sum-mertime. Day care for medium/large dogs is $25, $37 for 24 hours; rates are lower for small dogs; higher for extra-large dogs. Dogs must pass a two-hour free-play test to be admit-ted. Discounts offered for regulars, multiple-dog households, and Eastern State Dog Park members. Taxi service is available within an eight-mile radius for $8.

## UC Pet Tenders

(215) 990-6254
Philadelphia, PA
mkrull@earthlink.net
**Hours:** By Appt
**Payment:** Checks
**Price Range:** $$

UC Pet Tenders is run by Mark Krull, who has been walking Philly dogs for over three years. Mark has a second walker on staff, and between the two of them they usually have no problem accommodating last-minute requests — even on holidays. Walks are 15 minutes, which usually winds up being about a mile. One lunchtime walk is $12, but the bargain is two walks a day for $15 or three walks for $20, both packages include feeding. UC Pet Tenders will care for any breed as long as the dog isn't aggressive. Most of his clients are located in the University City area, though he does have a few customers in Center City.

# Chester, Delaware & Montgomery Counties

## ALTERNATIVE PRODUCTS/SERVICES

**All Neighborhoods**
Pickett, Kim
Veterinary Alternatives

**Havertown**
Superior Pet

**Newtown Square**
Delchester Discount Feed & Pet

**Wayne**
Braxton's Animal Works
Hunt, George, DVM

**Malvern**
Henley's Boutique for Dogs & Cats

**Narberth**
Main Line Pet Spa

## ANESTHESIA-FREE TEETH CLEANING

**Narberth**
Main Line Pet Spa

## ANIMAL HOSPITALS & VET CLINICS

**Ardmore**
Ardmore Animal Hospital
Ivens Veterinary Hospital

**Haverford**
Haverford Animal Hospital

**Havertown**
Havertown Animal Hospital

**King of Prussia**
Gulph Mills Veterinary Hospital

**Narberth**
Narberth Animal Hospital

**Newtown Square**
Colonial Animal Hospital

**Valley Forge**
Metropolitan Veterinary Associates & Emergency Services

**Wayne**
Hunt, George, DVM

# CAT SERVICES/PRODUCTS AVAILABLE

**All Neighborhoods**
Dr. Dogdirt Dog Waste Cleanup Service
Home and Pet Watch
Paws and Purrs Sitters
Veterinary Alternatives

**Ardmore**
Ardmore Animal Hospital
Pet Valu: Ardmore
Petco: Ardmore

**Blue Bell**
Pet Valu: Center Square

**Broomall**
PetSmart: Broomall

**Chadds Ford**
Concord Pet Foods & Supplies: Chadds Ford

**Clifton Heights**
Petco: Clifton Heights

**Devon**
PetSmart: Devon

**Dowington**
PetSmart: Exton

**Haverford**
Haverford Animal Hospital

**Havertown**
Havertown Animal Hospital

**Huntingdon Valley**
Pet Valu: Huntingdon Valley

**Jefferson**
Ruff Cuts

**Jenkintown**
Pet Valu: Jenkintown
PetSmart: Jenkintown

**King of Prussia**
Bow Wow Boutique
Petco: King of Prussia

**Malvern**
Henley's Boutique for Dogs & Cats
Petco: Malvern

**Maple Glen**
Pet Diner

**Narberth**
Narberth Animal Hosptial

**Montgomeryville**
Petco: Montgomeryville

**Norristown**
Pet Valu: Norristown

**North Wales**
PetSmart: North Wales

**Plymouth Meeting**
PetSmart: Plymouth Meeting

**Radnor**
Pet Valu: Chesterbrook

**Springfield**
Prince's Automative Repairs & Pet Goodies

**Trappe**
Petco: Trappe

**West Chester**
Applebrook Inn Pet Resort
Concord Pet Foods & Supplies: West Chester

**Willow Grove**
Petco: Willow Grove

## CITY DOG PICKS

**Chadds Ford**
Best Friends Pet Resort: Chadds Ford

**Frazer**
Great Valley Pet Hotel
Karen's K9 Care

**Malvern**
Henley's Boutique for Dogs & Cats

**Valley Forge**
Metropolitan Veterinary Associates & Emergency Services

**Wayne**
Hunt, George, DVM
Radnor Multi-Purpose Trail

## DOG BOARDING

**Ardmore**
Ivens Veterinary Hospital

**Chadds Ford**
Best Friends Pet Resort: Chadds Ford

**Devon**
Devon Boarding and Grooming

**Frazer**
Great Valley Pet Hotel
Karen's K9 Care

**Havertown**
Havertown Animal Hospital

**King of Prussia**
Bow Wow Boutique
Gulph Mills Veterinary Hospital

**Malvern**
Buckwalter Kennels Inc

**Narberth**
Narberth Animal Hospital

**Newtown Square**
Colonial Animal Hospital

**Ridley Park**
Frame's Kennels

**Wayne**
Hunt, George, DVM

**West Chester**
Applebrook Inn Pet Resort

# DOG DAY CARE

**Chadds Ford**
Best Friends Pet Resort: Chadds Ford

**Frazer**
Great Valley Pet Hotel
Karen's K9 Care

**Jeffersonville**
Ruff Cuts

**King of Prussia**
Bow Wow Boutique

**Narberth**
Narberth Animal Hospital

**West Chester**
Applebrook Inn Pet Resort

# DOG GROOMING

**All Neighborhoods**
Bark and Park Mobile Pet Grooming Salon

**Ardmore**
Petco: Ardmore

**Brookhaven**
Peaceable Grooming

**Broomall**
PetSmart: Broomall

**Bryn Mawr**
Kimie's Animal Art

**Chadds Ford**
Best Friends Pet Resort: Chadds Ford

**Clifton Heights**
Petco: Clifton Heights

**Devon**
Devon Boarding and Grooming
PetSmart: Devon

**Downington**
PetSmart: Exton

**Frazer**
Great Valley Pet Hotel

**Holmes**
Diamond Dogs Grooming

**Jeffersonville**
Ruff Cuts

**Jenkintown**
PetSmart: Jenkintown

**King of Prussia**
Bow Wow Boutique
Petco: King of Prussia

**Montgomeryville**
Petco: Montgomeryville

**Narberth**
Main Line Pet Spa
Narberth Animal Hospital

**Newtown Square**
Petagree

**North Wales**
PetSmart: North Wales

**Plymouth Meeting**
PetSmart: Plymouth Meeting

**West Chester**
Applebrook Inn Pet Resort

# DOG PARKS & TRAILS

**Horsham**
Graeme Park

**Radnor**
Harford Dog Park
Radnor Multi-Purpose Trail

# DOG TRAINING

**All Neighborhoods**
Main Line Dog Training/Pam Coath

**Broomall**
PetSmart: Broomall

**Devon**
PetSmart: Devon

**Downington**
PetSmart: Exton

**Haverford**
Philadelphia Dog Training Club, Inc.

**Jeffersonville**
Ruff Cuts

**Jenkintown**
PetSmart: Jenkintown

**King of Prussia**
Perfect Pooch

**Newton Square**
Dog Training School of Delaware County

**North Wales**
PetSmart: North Wales

**Plymouth Meeting**
PetSmart: Plymouth Meeting

**Wayne**
Braxton's Animal Works

# DOG WALKING/PET SITTING

**All Neighborhoods**
Creature Comforts
Dog Gone It
Home and Pet Watch
In-Demand In Home Pet Sitting
Paw Prints Barkery
Paws and Purrs Sitters
Pet Nanny **(S)**
PetCare Group **(S)**

# LOW-COST VACCINATION CLINICS

**Ardmore**
Petco: Ardmore
**Clifton Heights**
Petco: Clifton Heights

**Downington**
PetSmart: Exton

**Jenkintown**
PetSmart: Jenkintown

**King Of Prussia**
Petco: King of Prussia

**Malvern**
Petco: Malvern

**Montgomeryville**
Petco: Montgomeryville

**Plymouth Meeting**
PetSmart: Plymouth Meeting

**Trappe**
Petco: Trappe

**Willow Grove**
Petco: Willow Grove

# ON-SITE PET ADOPTIONS

**Ardmore**
Petco: Ardmore

**Broomall**
PetSmart: Broomall

**Clifton Heights**
Petco: Clifton Heights

**Devon**
PetSmart: Devon

**Downington**
PetSmart: Exton

**Frazer**
Karen's K9 Care

**Jenkintown**
PetSmart: Jenkintown

**King Of Prussia**
Petco: King of Prussia

**Malvern**
Petco: Malvern

**Montgomeryville**
Petco: Montgomeryville

**North Wales**
PetSmart: North Wales

**Plymouth Meeting**
PetSmart: Plymouth Meeting

**Trappe**
Petco: Trappe

# PET-SUPPLY STORES

**All Neighborhoods**
Paw Prints Barkery

**Ardmore**
Petco: Ardmore

**Bala Cynwyd**
Pet Valu: Ardmore

**Blue Bell**
Pet Valu: Center Square

**Broomall**
PetSmart: Broomall

**Chadds Ford**
Concord Pet Foods & Supplies: Chadds Ford

**Clifton Heights**
Petco: Clifton Heights

**Devon**
PetSmart: Devon

**Downington**
PetSmart: Exton

**Havertown**
Superior Pet

**Huntingdon Valley**
Pet Valu: Huntingdon Valley

**Jenkintown**
Pet Valu: Jenkintown
PetSmart: Jenkintown

**King of Prussia**
Bow Wow Boutique
Petco: King of Prussia

**Malvern**
Henley's Boutique for Dogs & Cats
Petco: Malvern

**Maple Glen**
Pet Diner

**Montgomeryville**
Petco: Montgomeryville

**Narberth**
Spot's — The Place for Paws

**Newtown Square**
Delchester Discount Feed & Pet

**Norristown**
Pet Valu: Norristown

**North Wales**
PetSmart: North Wales

**Plymouth Meeting**
PetSmart: Plymouth Meeting

**Radnor**
Pet Valu: Chesterbrook

**Springfield**
Prince's Automotive Repairs & Pet Goodies

**Trappe**
Petco: Trappe

**Wayne**
Bone Appetite, The: Wayne
Braxton's Animal Works
Peaches & Gable

**West Chester**
Concord Pet Foods & Supplies: West Chester

**Willow Grove**
Petco: Willow Grove

# PHOTOGRAPHY/PAINTINGS

**Ardmore**
Petco: Ardmore

**Hershey**
Animal Instincts Pet Photography and Digital Imaging

**Malvern**
Petco: Malvern

**Montgomeryville**
Petco: Montgomeryville

**Newtown Square**
Facenda, Paul Photography, Inc.

**Trappe**
Petco: Trappe

# POOP-REMOVAL SERVICE

Clean Scoop Dog Waste Removal Service
Dr. Dogdirt Dog Waste Cleanup Service
TMC Dog Waste Disposal Service

# SELF-SERVE DOG GROOMING

**Wynnewood**
Petco: Ardmore

# SHUTTLE SERVICE

**All Neighborhoods**
Creature Comforts
Pet Nanny
PetCare Group

# General Listings

## Animal Instincts Pet Photography and Digital Imaging

(717) 533-4013
1538 E Derry Rd, (@ Howard Ave)
Hershey, PA  17033
**Hours:** By Appt
**Payment:** Credit Cards, Checks
**Price Range:**  $$$

If you're looking for something a little more formal than your point-and-shoot can deliver, you may want to call in the experts at Animal Instincts. Ever accommodating of the working set, Animal Instincts not only works weekends, but will also travel far from their Hershey studio to backyard locations for outdoorsy sky-as-backdrop pet photos. Of course, if you're looking for a straight-up portrait, you can bring your dog to their studios. Prefer a more artistic memento of your pet? Artist Loreen Adams will do a painting of your pup from your favorite photo for your family gallery.

## Applebrook Inn Pet Resort

(610) 692-7178
1691 W Strasburg Rd, (W of Broad Run Rd)
West Chester, PA  19382
**Hours:** Mon – Sat 10 AM – 6 PM
         Closed for drop off/pick up between 12 PM – 4 PM
**Payment:** Credit Cards, Checks
**Price Range:**  $$

Applebrook is a great place for your dog to hang out when you're on vacation. Grouped by compatibility, dogs enjoy free play in seven fenced-in runs as well as a spacious playroom that opens into a yard. Pups spend mealtime and bedtime in their own indoor/outdoor run. You can bring your own, but bedding and food are provided (toys are also welcome). Daycare is $12 per day; boarding is $18 per night. There is a small surcharge ($1 per administration) for medications. Grooming (starting at $20) is also available. Dogs are partially dried in no-heat cage dryers, then finished by hand. Call three weeks ahead for holiday bookings; otherwise, a week will suffice.

# Ardmore Animal Hospital

(610) 642-1160
24 E Athens Ave
(@ Rittenhouse Pl)
Ardmore, PA  19003
www.ardmoreah.com

**Hours:** Mon 8 AM – 6 PM, Tue – Thu 8 AM – 8 PM
Fri 8 AM – 6 PM
Sat 8 AM – 12 PM

**Payment:** Credit Cards, Checks

**Price Range:**  $$

A staff of five veterinarians and two on-call specialists care for small animals — including chinchillas and hamsters — at this converted home in residential Ardmore. They offer general checkups, vaccinations, spaying/neutering, nutritional counseling and other preventative treatments. Ardmore also performs laser surgery, X-rays, blood testing, and nursing care. They no longer offer boarding (except for cats) or grooming. Clients can order prescriptions and download forms on the hospital's Web site. For after-hours emergency service, Ardmore refers people to Old Marple Veterinary Center or West Chester Emergency Animal Clinic.

# Bark and Park Mobile Pet Grooming Salon

(800) 383-6902

**Hours:** By Appt

**Payment:** Checks

**Price Range:**  $$$

Well-heeled Main Line and suburban dog owners relish the convenience of this pet salon on wheels. While Bark and Park's aromatherapy and luxury whirlpool offerings have their admirers, most customers prefer having less glamorous pet maintenance tasks like sanitary shaving, hand scissoring, dental scaling, or tick removal done in the comfort of a grooming van parked just outside their home. Weekend and evening appointments are popular, as is the company's refusal to use tranquilizers. Hit the ATM if you're interested; first-time customers must pay cash.

## Best Friends Pet Resort: Chadds Ford

(610) 459-2724
3914 Pyle Rd
(@ Trotters Lea Ln)
Chadds Ford, PA 19317
www.bestfriendspetcare.com
**Hours:** Mon – Thu 8 AM – 6 PM
Fri – Sat 8 AM – 5 PM
Sun 3 PM – 6 PM
**Payment:** Credit Cards, Checks
**Price Range:** $$

Employees are helpful and knowledgeable at this popular chain, which offers a full range of services. Prices for day care ($15) and boarding ($24 to $30) are quite reasonable, but beware of extras, like playtime and meds, that can drive the fees way up over an extended stay. They offer grooming amenities, including manicures and moisturizing treatments. Forced-air hand dryers and no-heat cage dryers are used. Be sure to ask about the Shedicure — a treatment that combines the FURminator and a carding process, it can reduce shedding up to 80 percent.

## Bone Appetite, The: Wayne

(610) 995-2663
122 E Lancaster Ave
(between Louella & S Waybe Aves)
Wayne, PA 19087
www.theboneappetite.com
**Hours:** Mon – Sat 10 AM – 5:30 PM
**Payment:** Credit Cards, Checks
**Price Range:** $$$

This chic doggie bakery has two locations: one right on the Main Line, proudly perched among some of the area's smartest retail space, and another in historic Chestnut Hill. Despite its swank company and polished appearance, the friendly staff is down to earth and eager to pamper your pet with generous portions of free samples. Offerings include homemade bakery treats, birthday cakes, custom collars, custom painted bowls, complete with your pup's paw print, and pet beds in your choice of fabrics. Add a lot of pick-me-ups for impromptu gift giving and dog spoiling, and you start to feel Bone Appetite's fresh-baked, wholesome appeal.

## Bow Wow Boutique

(610) 265-3646
132 Hansen Access Rd
(@ Henderson Rd)
King of Prussia, PA  19406
**Hours:** Mon, Sat 9 AM – 4 PM
Tue – Fri 7:15 AM – 6 PM
**Payment:** Credit Cards
**Price Range:**  $$

This one-stop dog shop offers supplies and accessories, as well as day care ($12/day), boarding ($20/night), and grooming (starting at $60). Boutique offerings include rawhides, treats, clothes, beds, toys, and leashes. Day-care dogs are separated by size, with small dogs in an area the size of a two-car garage, larger dogs in a carport-type structure. The staff makes sure dogs are fed and taken outside three times a day. However, there is no night-time supervision. First-timers take note: if your pup needs a bath or a clip, be sure to call ahead; grooming is by appointment only. Forced-air and cage dryers are used. Keep an eye out, Hansen Access Road is easy to miss.

## Braxton's Animal Works

(610) 688-0769
620 West Lancaster Ave
(between Old Eagle School Rd & Old Sugartown Rd)
Wayne, PA  19087
www.braxtons.com
**Hours:** Mon – Sat 9 AM – 7 PM
Sun 10 AM – 5 PM
**Payment:** Credit Cards, Checks
**Price Range:**  $$

Since it opened its doors in 1938, this Main Line institution has been owned and operated by the same family for three generations. Many of its customers are third-generation as well — because if there's one thing Braxton's understands and values, it's customer loyalty. Their Pet Pass program gives faithful customers cash rewards and sneak peeks at new products. Over the years Braxton's shelves have grown to accommodate national and specialty brands, as well as organic and high-tech products. And you can still find perennial favorites like the outdoor Dogloo. Training offered on-site.

## Buckwalter Kennels Inc

(610) 644-6918
106 Lancaster Ave
(@ Conestoga Rd)
Malvern, PA 19355
**Hours:** Mon – Fri 8 AM – 6 PM
       Sat 9 AM – 4 PM
**Payment:** Credit Cards, Checks
**Price Range:** $$

This family-operated boarding kennel is now in its 50th year. With the owner living on-site, it's the next best thing to an in-home sitter. Feel free to bring favorite chews, toys, and whatever else makes your pup feel at home — even his bed! The house chow is a commercial-brand dog food. However, you can BYO for no extra charge. Rates are $18 per day for small/medium-sized dogs, $22 for dogs over 50 pounds. Pre-pay and show up between 1 PM and 2 PM for Sunday pickups. In winter, you will usually have no problem getting a space with a day's notice. During the holidays and summertime, two weeks' notice is advised.

## Clean Scoop Dog Waste Removal Service

(215) 887-7698
www.cleanscoop.net
**Hours:** By Appt
**Payment:** Credit Cards, Checks
**Price Range:** $

These pooper-scoopers scoop lawns and yards in Radnor, Villanova, and Gladwyne. Based near Fort Washington, they won't travel beyond a 20-mile radius unless they have several customers. Their services can be utilized weekly, monthly, biweekly, bimonthly, or one time only. Waste is double-bagged and trashed on-site. A first-time cleaning fee for a quarter-acre is $25 for the first half-hour, then $10 for each additional 15 minutes. After that, you can count on paying somewhere around $10 per dog, per week. Believe it or not, they offer gift certificates — perhaps the perfect present for the pup-loving pragmatist in your life.

## Colonial Animal Hospital
(610) 353-1881
4 South Newtown St Rd
(@ Westchester Pike)
Newtown Square, PA 19073
**Hours:** Mon, Fri 9 AM – 5 PM,
Tue – Thu 9 AM – 7 PM, Sat 9 AM – 12 PM
**Payment:** Credit Cards, Checks
**Price Range:** $$

Colonial Animal Hospital owner and resident vet Dan Rufus, DVM, is like the family doctor — only his patients are limited to the four-legged set. Centrally located, his practice stands out for the efficient service it provides to the area's animals. A routine exam will run you $39. Colonial also offers comfortable boarding, complete with three breaks in the exercise run each day, for existing clients. Dogs under 50 pounds are $16 a day, dogs over 50 pounds are $18 a day. The hospital recommends you BYO food to minimize the disruption to your dog's daily regimen. Dogs are not supervised at night.

## Concord Pet Foods & Supplies
**Hours:** Mon – Sat 9 AM – 9 PM
Sun 10 AM – 5 PM
**Payment:** Credit Cards, Checks
**Price Range:** $/$$/$$$
www.concordpet.com

## Concord Pet Foods & Supplies: Chadds Ford
(610) 459-5990
291 Wilmington W Chester Pike
(@ Smith Bridge Rd)
Chadds Ford, PA 19317

## Concord Pet Foods & Supplies: West Chester
(610) 701-9111
804 E Market St
(between Westtown Rd & Wilson Ave)
West Chester, PA 19382

Concord takes one-stop shopping to a whole new level — stocking everything from foods (Wellness, Innova, and Natura) to Wee Wee pads ($40 for 100) to Outward Hound life jackets. They also have a full line of Booda toys, joint supplements, car seats, brushes, and shampoos, as well as Nylabone chews ($2 to $5 each). And if you feel like turning your backyard into a nature sanctuary, they also offer supplies for squirrels, deer, birds, and rodents, as well as items for reptiles, pigs, and, of course, dogs. You can shop online or head to one of their stores to take advantage of their excellent customer service.

## Creature Comforts

(610) 642-2287
**Hours:** By Appt
**Payment:** Checks
**Price Range:** $$

Voted Best of Philly by *Philadelphia* magazine in 2004, you can count on Creature Comforts to keep your pet comfy while you are away. Owners/operators Andrea and Steven Sergio keep a close eye on their charges. They've been known to catch medical problems before their dogs' owners even noticed something was amiss. Sitting and walking fees begin at $15 per half-hour. They also offer pet transportation within their service area, which runs from Villanova to Bala Cynwyd.

## Delchester Discount Feed & Pet

(610) 356-8350
32 S Newtown Street Rd
(between Reese St & Mary Jane Ln)
Newtown Square, PA 19073
**Hours:** Mon – Fri 10 AM – 6 PM
Sat 9 AM – 5 PM
**Payment:** Credit Cards, Checks
**Price Range:** $$$

With human-grade, all-natural goodies spilling off the shelves, this high-end, healthy "niche" pet store is an organic extravaganza for dogs. Delchester stocks a variety of hard-to-find products like the organic dog food Karma (a 15-pound bag is $45). You'll also find a great selection of all-natural bones as well as toys, grooming tools, and other must-haves for your pup. Park in the back.

## Devon Boarding and Grooming

(610) 687-0211
81 Lancaster Ave
(@ S Valley Forge Rd)
Devon, PA 19333
**Hours:** Mon 7:30 AM – 8 PM, Tue – Thu 7:30 AM – 6 PM
Fri 7:30 AM – 8 PM, Sat 8 AM – 5 PM
**Payment:** Credit Cards, Checks
**Price Range:** $$

Located inside a veterinary office, Devon offers expert
grooming services for dogs and cats. This team of groomers,
which boasts 15-year veteran Sue, offers great cuts and a full
compliment of medicated and hypoallergenic shampoos. Basic
grooming ($63) includes a soothing hand-washing and con-
ditioning, and temperature-controlled cage drying. Boarding
is also available — unlike many veterinary boarding facilities,
Devon offers outdoor runs so dogs get some daytime play.
Rates are $17 per day for dogs less than 45 pounds; $22 for
dogs over 45 pounds. Bonus: there is a vet tech on-site at all
times. Boarding and grooming are both by appointment only.

## Diamond Dogs Grooming

(610) 532-4566
2021 MacDade Blvd
(@ Parker Ave)
Holmes, PA 19043
**Hours:** Tue – Fri 8 AM – 5 PM
**Payment:** Credit Cards, Cash
**Price Range:** $$

No dog is turned away from this family-owned and -operated
grooming facility. They accept all sizes and breeds — even
if your precious pup is a pit bull. Grooming includes a full
bath, nail clipping, comb out, and fluff dry. Custom cuts are
available by request. Remember to mention their Web site
to save 10 percent off your dog's services. Appointments are
recommended, but walk-ins can frequently be accommodated,
provided you arrive before 1 PM.

# Dog Gone It

(610) 517-3886

jdoggoneit@aol.com

**Hours:** By Appt

**Payment:** Checks

**Price Range:** $$

If this likeable sitter were writing a personal ad, it might read, "Attractive, responsible, mature male seeks dog for long walks and mutual affection." With 16 years experience in a variety of animal care positions (mostly at veterinary clinics and kennels), Jon charges $15 for 20 – 25 minutes of quality time with your dog. Feeding, walking, medication, and cleanup are included. He says dog-aggressive dogs are no problem, since walking dogs individually is standard procedure. However, if your dog gets along well with others, group walks are also an option. Call for a no-commitment free consultation. References provided upon request.

# Dog Training School of Delaware County

(610) 356-2822

Paxon Hollow Rd & Palmers Mill Rd

Newton Square, PA  19073

**Hours:** Tue – Fri 7 AM – 8 PM

Sat 9:30 AM – 12 PM

**Payment:** Checks

**Price Range:** $

Having transformed over 140,000 rambunctious pups into well-mannered dogs this reputable training center is well-equipped to teach your dog good behavior. These experienced trainers — there's 50 years of experience under the Dog Training School's collective belt — use the tried-and-true training collar. Puppies under six months of age start with a personal consultation, dogs six months and older, begin with a private one-hour class with the head trainer ($50), then take ten follow-up classes in a group environment ($70 for all 10). Other offerings include novice, utility, and open classes. The entire family is strongly encouraged to attend all classes.

## Dr. Dogdirt Dog Waste Cleanup Service
(610) 932-8574
**Hours:** By Appt
**Payment:** Checks
**Price Range:** $$

Dr. Dogdirt serves Delaware County and southern Chester County. His rates are based on the size of your yard: anything under a quarter-acre is $8 per weekly visit; an acre is $12 per weekly visit. One-time cleanings usually cost a minimum of $25, but if the yard hasn't been cleaned in a while it could cost more. Trash will not be removed, though owner Bob is flexible about removing other items (when possible) and on occasion he has raked leaves from yards. He also cleans litter boxes.

## Facenda, Paul Photography, Inc.
(610) 356-5382
43 Bishop Hollow Rd
(@ School Ln)
Newtown Square, PA  19073
www.facendaphoto.com
**Hours:** By Appt
**Payment:** Credit Cards, Checks
**Price Range:** $$$

Selected Best of the Main Line by *Main Line Today* two years in a row, photographer Paul Facenda uses his gorgeously restored Victorian home as the backdrop for his photos of person and hound. And he's great with the ensemble holiday photo, using a variety of attention-getting tricks to capture both pup and person. Sitting fees begin at $100 for indoor; $138 for outdoor; and $165 for off-site shoots. Samples of his work can be found on his Web site, along with samples of his commercial and wedding photography.

## Frame's Kennels

(610) 521-1123
1119 Haverford Rd
(@ Bonsel Rd)
Ridley Park, PA 19078
**Hours:** Mon – Sat 8 AM – 7 PM
**Payment:** Cash
**Price Range:** $$

This low-cost, bare-bones boarding kennel is located in a converted house. For $15 a day, your dog will have his own 6 x 8-foot indoor kennel that is connected to an outdoor run. Dogs aren't walked and don't mix company, so this boarding facility is adequate for the low-maintenance, antisocial pup that doesn't require any exercise. The house chow is Pedigree, wet and dry, but you're welcome to provide your own food, which they'll feed at no additional charge.

## Graeme Park

(215) 343-0965
859 County Line Rd
(@ Rte 611)
Horsham, PA 19044
www.ushistory.org/graeme
**Hours:** Wed – Sat 10 AM – 4 PM
　　　　　Sun 12 PM – 4 PM
**Payment:** Free

Nature lovers, hikers, and tourists share this beautiful 44-acre historic park with dog owners, pet sitters, and of course, plenty of pups. The park, which is home to wild animals — deer, wild turkeys and hawks abound — is open to visitors year round. The park also boasts the Keith House, an 18th-century mansion that was home to colonial governor Sir William Keith. Dogs must remain on leash at all times, and all food and waste must be properly disposed of. Built on wetlands, Graeme Park can get very muddy at certain times of year so be sure to bring towels. There is no entrance fee unless the park is hosting a special event.

## Great Valley Pet Hotel
(610) 296-8330
25 Davis Ave
(@ Lancaster Pike)
Frazer, PA 19355
www.greatvalleypethotel.com
**Hours:** Mon – Fri 6:30 AM – 6:30 PM
**Payment:** Credit Cards, Checks
**Price Range:** $$

This idyllic two-acre doggie getaway, complete with an ivy-covered country home-gone-kennel, is only moments from the hubbub of suburbia. Offerings include boarding ($18 to $20), Doggie Day Camp ($22), and grooming. Day camp attendees enjoy group free play in a fenced-in pasture, with a break for naptime from noon until 2 PM. Indoor and outdoor ramps make it easy for seniors to navigate the facility and join in the fun. Grooming services are a la carte, with bathing starting at $15 and full grooming starting at $30. Note: there is a $10 additional charge for boarded dogs to participate in day camp. Multiple-dog and package discounts are available.

## Gulph Mills Veterinary Hospital
(610) 265-6044
395 S Gulph Rd
(between Brooks & W Church Rds)
King of Prussia, PA 19406
**Hours:** Mon, Tue, Thu 9 AM – 7 PM
Wed, Sat 9 AM – 12 PM
Fri 9 AM – 6 PM
**Payment:** Credit Cards, Checks
**Price Range:** $$$

If you can deal with the popularity — appointments require two-weeks notice — and the price — a routine exam is $42 — then this service-oriented animal hospital is simply superb. The staff is outgoing and caring, and the sole presiding doctor does everything from checkups and vaccinations to surgeries. An ophthalmologist and radiologist are also on call. For emergencies, the doctor can be reached by pager 24/7. Limited boarding for pre-existing clients is also available.

# Harford Dog Park

(610) 688-5600
260 Gulph Creek Rd
(Across from the Creutzburg Center)
Radnor, PA 19087
**Hours:** Every Day: Sunrise to Sunset
**Payment:** Free

This park, which is for residents of Radnor Township only, features sprawling hills of open grass where you'll find several dogs congregating at any given point during the day. It is especially bustling on Sunday afternoons. For the most part, dogs all stay in the center area, running around and playing off-leash. There are some benches on the edges of the park, and a doggie-fountain for thirsty pups. Beware: the park is not fenced-in, so your dog needs to be under voice control. Harford is located up a long driveway off of Gulph Road, across from the Creutzburg Center.

# Haverford Animal Hospital

(610) 525-1211
517 W Lancaster Ave
(between Tenmore & Old Lancaster Rds)
Haverford, PA 19041
**Hours:** Mon – Tue, Thu – Fri 9 AM – 8 PM
　　　　 Wed, Sat 9 AM – 12 PM
**Payment:** Credit Cards, Checks
**Price Range:** $$

Winner of the 2001 *Main Line Life* Reader's Choice Award for Best Veterinarian, Haverford Animal Hospital has served Main Line and Philadelphia pets for five decades. The facility, which sits in a two-story tan stucco building with a bold red sign, houses Reginald L. Royster, DVM, and his enthusiastic team of vet techs. They pride themselves on their state-of-the-art surgical suite, radiology department, and laboratory. Basic exams, spay/neuter procedures, and routine small-animal veterinary medicine are Haverford's stock in trade. Evening hours make weekday visits manageable. You can order pet-related products and refill prescriptions and medications on the user-friendly Web site.

## Havertown Animal Hospital
(610) 449-5100
1200 West Chester Pike
(@ Pinzon Ave)
Havertown, PA  19083
www.havertownvet.com
**Hours:** Mon, Fri 8:30 AM – 5:45 PM
　　　　　Tue – Thu 2 PM – 5:45 PM, Sat 8 AM – 11:45 AM
**Payment:** Credit Cards, Checks
**Price Range:**  $$
A sole practitioner with an exceptional support staff, Dr. Croce founded this state-of-the-art facility, which offers both X-rays and lab work on-site, in 2001. Services range from routine exams ($34), to emergency surgery, to dental care. Tuesday and Thursday mornings are reserved for scheduled surgeries, but clients are easily accommodated during Havertown's otherwise normal hours. Emergencies are referred to the Veterinary Hospital at the University of Pennsylvania. The clinic provides boarding for clients only. Boarded pups are kept in individual kennels or runs (smaller dogs cost $13/day). Dogs are supervised and walked three times a day, but left alone at night.

## Henley's Boutique for Dogs & Cats
(610) 296-0100
113 E King St
(@ Bridgetown Pike)
Malvern, PA  19355
**Hours:** Tue – Thu 10 AM – 6 PM, Fri 10 AM – 6:30 PM
　　　　　Sat 9 AM – 5 PM, Sun 11 AM – 3 PM
**Payment:** Credit Cards, Checks
**Price Range:**  $$$
Perfect for preppy puppies, Henley's offerings include pink-and-green, candy-striped, and tartan collars, all available with matching leads, sized to fit teacup chihuahuas, Newfoundlands and everything in between. You'll also find a wide array of organic biscuits, vitamins, and more shampoos than most beauty salons carry. Snappy coats and sweaters are available in all colors and styles. And if you're not satisfied with Henley's bed selection, you may bring your own fabric and they will have one custom-made. Bring along your tired sweaters and worn-out collars — there's a basket at the door for donations that go to underprivileged pets.

## Home and Pet Watch

(610) 566-4558
**Hours:** Mon – Sun 8 AM – 8 PM
**Payment:** Checks
**Price Range:** $

Word is, Rich is reliable. His trustworthy pet-sitting team has served the Media, Newtown Square, Drexel Hill, and Havertown areas for 12 years. At $14 a visit, your dog will be walked, fed, and brushed. You can also request plant watering as well as mail and newspaper collection. Visits usually last between 20 and 30 minutes. Rich and company are not just for hound and home, they will also tend to fish, ferrets, cats, and any other animal you consider a pet. Home and Pet Watch is bonded, insured, and a member of PSI.

## Hunt, George, DVM

(610) 688-1776
405 W Wayne Ave
(@ Conestoga Rd)
Wayne, PA 19087
**Hours:** Mon, Wed – Fri 8:30 AM – 6 PM
　　　　Tue 8:30 AM – 8 PM
　　　　Sat 8:30 AM – 12 PM
**Payment:** Credit Cards, Checks
**Price Range:** $$$

Located in the heart of South Wayne, near the Radnor Bike Trail, George Hunt, DVM, has long tended to the area's veterinary needs. And his practice now offers boarding as well in a new climate-controlled building. The medical staff offers traditional veterinary services and state-of-the-art care, as well as alternative treatments such as acupuncture. Clients praise the extraordinarily compassionate care afforded their animals here. Bereaved pet owners receive a handwritten letter, in which this caring vet reviews his personal history with the animal.

## In-Demand In Home Pet Sitting
(215) 878-6108
PO Box 2563
Bala Cynwyd, PA 19004
www.indemandpetsitting.com
**Hours:** By Appt
**Payment:** Credit Cards, Checks
**Price Range:** $$
With online reservation and payment options, In-Demand Pet
Sitting, in business since 1987 and boasting an eight-person
staff, makes coordinating pet care a breeze. In addition to the
usual feeding- and walking-type duties, sitters will also bring in
the mail and leave you a detailed note about the day's events
for $22 per half-hour visit. Great for special needs dogs, the
staff is trained to give injections and administer IVs. And if you
run out of chow, they'll even do a pet-food run. If you buy "in
bulk," you'll get a better rate. Serving Ardmore, Bala Cynwyd,
Belmont Hills, Havertown, Merion, Narberth, Penn Valley,
Villanova, and Wynnewood.

## Ivens Veterinary Hospital
(610) 649-4242
60 Haverford Rd
(between Ardmore & College Aves)
Ardmore, PA 19003
**Hours:** Mon – Fri 9 AM – 6 PM
　　　　Sat 9 AM – 12 PM
**Payment:** Credit Cards, Checks
**Price Range:** $$
With the owner of the practice living on the grounds and three
additional veterinarians on staff, this small-animal hospital
provides personalized care with a smile. A routine exam will
run you $50, $80 if your pup is getting vaccinated at the same
time. Ivens performs numerous surgeries. However, they refer
out for cardiology, orthopedics, and anything else they are
unable to handle in-house. The small building that houses the
veterinary offices belies the size of the kennel which can hold
up to 60 dogs. (Granted, all dogs must be under 20 pounds.)
Appointments can be scheduled with a couple of days' notice.

## Karen's K9 Care

(610) 725-8973
457 & 459 Lancaster Ave
(between Rte 457 & Rte 459)
Frazer, PA 19355
www.karensk9care.com
**Hours:** Mon – Fri 6:15 AM – 7 PM
Sat 8 AM – 5 PM,
Sun 8 AM – 12 PM
**Payment:** Credit Cards
**Price Range:** $$

Karen's philosophy that "a tired dog is a good dog" led her to open K9 Care. The facility boasts indoor and outdoor runs and an outside playground that is complete with a jungle gym. Inside, there are plenty of blankets for pups to rest on. The rate is $25 per day, with discounts for weekly and monthly packages. Pups not picked up by 7 PM must spend the night ($30). Karen's holds on-site adoptions and fosters pups for Brookline Labrador Retriever Rescue. Karen also runs an Animal Assisted Activities (AAA) group that goes into local assisted-living homes. (All dogs must be Canine Good Citizen-certified to participate in AAA.)

## Kimie's Animal Art

(610) 527-4677
839 W Lancaster Ave
(@ Central Ave)
Bryn Mawr, PA 19010
**Hours:** By Appt
**Payment:** Credit Cards, Checks
**Price Range:** $$$

Located in the heart of Bryn Mawr's shopping district, business at Kimie's Animal Art is always buzzing. From the name, you'd think this was a portrait studio, but rather, it's a pet salon that specializes in particularly chic cuts and clips. Offering a choice of shampoos including antibacterial and oatmeal, this bright, spacious shop welcomes all breeds, plus the family cat, too. Reservations must be made at least a week in advance. Street parking is difficult, but you can drop your pooch off at the back door. The alley's one way — turn off Morton.

## Main Line Dog Training/Pam Coath

(610) 688-2277
**Hours:** By Appt
**Payment:** Checks
**Price Range:** $$

With treats at the ready to reward good behavior, Main Line trainer Pam Coath uses positive reinforcement to train her canine pupils. She will sometimes use a clicker for training, but warns that they aren't a good idea in homes with small children. She teaches private basic-obedience lessons ($75 for a 90-minute session in your home) and will also tackle such issues as jumping, barking, chewing, and housebreaking. She works with all breeds, but especially loves training toy breeds and puppies, and will occasionally board both in her home. APDT certified.

## Main Line Pet Spa

(610) 668-7704
944 Montgomery Ave
(between Gordon Ave & Old Gulph Rd)
Narberth, PA 19072
**Hours:** Tue – Fri 8:15 AM – 5 PM
Sat 8:30 AM – 5 PM
**Payment:** Credit Cards
**Price Range:** $

Medicated and organic shampoos abound in this snazzy salon, where a bath, brush, and wash starts at only $25. Book your pup for the popular tea-tree-oil shampoo treatment, de rigueur for any dog diva. Most dogs are dried by hand with forced-air dryers, but sensitive types can be dried with no-heat cage dryers. The salon welcomes all breeds and will do custom cuts. Nail trims, tooth brushing, and ear cleaning are also available. The Main Line Pet Spa hopes to expand its services in the near future to include canine massage services as well as a dog day care. Appointments should be booked at least a week in advance.

## Metropolitan Veterinary Associates & Emergency Services

(610) 666-1050
915 Trooper Rd
(in the Valley Forge Corporate Center)
Valley Forge, PA 19482
www.metro-vet.com
**Hours:** Mon – Thu 8 AM – 6 PM, Fri 8 AM – 6:15 PM
       **Emergency Services:** Every Day 24 Hours
**Payment:** Credit Cards, Checks
**Price Range:** $$$

A Mayo Clinic for dogs and other pets, this specialty hospital usually sees patients upon referral from their primary veterinarian. The hospital offers around-the-clock care with areas of expertise including cardiology, dentistry/oral surgery, dermatology, internal medicine, neurology, ophthalmology, radiology, and surgery (soft tissue/orthopedic/neurosurgery). Except for emergencies, appointments are required. Methods of payment vary according to the doctor providing the service, but written estimates are given during the first evaluation. The emergency hotline number is (610) 666-0914.

## Narberth Animal Hospital

(610) 664-4114
815 Montgomery Ave
(between Haverford Ave & Iona Ave)
Narberth, PA 19026
**Hours:** Mon – Wed 9 AM – 8 PM, Thu – Fri 9 AM – 5 PM
      Sat 9 AM – 12 PM
**Payment:** Credit Cards
**Price Range:** $$

This small veterinary hospital, which is home to the venerable Edward Scanlon, DVM, who just published a book about his career in animal service entitled *Animal Patients*, provides patients with top-notch treatment. They offer standard medical services (a routine exam costs $50), along with bathing, boarding, and day care. The hospital accepts emergency patients during business hours (after hours, they'll refer you to Metropolitan Animal Hospital). A member of the multicounty Spayed Club, a nonprofit effort to reduce pet overpopulation, Narberth is one of the few participating facilities to specialize in feral cats. The entrance is located just off Montgomery Avenue.

## Paw Prints Barkery and Pet Sitting

(610) 668-7730
www.pawprintsbarkery.com
**Hours:** By Appt
**Payment:** Credit Cards
**Price Range:** $$

Paw Prints is a one-stop pet-sitting and treat-making factory. Audrey Scheier, owner and chef of this popular five-year-old business, farms out professional sitters to folks in the Main Line area. For $15 a visit, your pup will get walked, fed, and if necessary, medicated. Paw Prints will also take care of cats, fish, birds, and rabbits. And if your dog has an appointment and you can't play chauffeur, they offer shuttle services as well. You can order their signature treats from your sitter or at the online store. Popular items include Snicker Poodles, Boney Bon-Bons, and the Peamutt Butter Hearts ($15 for a half-pound).

## Paws and Purrs Sitters

(610) 874-4075
http://pawsandpurrssitters.com
**Hours:** By Appt
**Payment:** Checks
**Price Range:** $$

Paws and Purrs owner Fran Danish — with her short blond hair and leather jacket — may look a little more rock and roll than canine caretaker extraordinaire, but she has an excellent reputation among Philadelphia's four-legged housebound set. After a trial meeting with you and your pet, Fran or one of her employees will step in when you need to step out. Standard visits include walking, feeding, and playtime. Other offerings include cleaning litter boxes, giving pups meds or injections, bringing in the mail, taking out the trash, and shuttle service. Each visit is topped off with a personalized note. Serving Delaware County, Center City, South Philly, and Newton Square.

## Peaceable Grooming

(610) 874-7040
4011 Edgmont Ave
(between Radio Park Ln & Brookhaven Rd)
Brookhaven, PA 19015
**Hours:** Tue – Sat 7 AM – 2 PM
**Payment:** Checks
**Price Range:** $$

This small, friendly dogs-only salon books up fast, so all grooming appointments must be made at least two weeks in advance. You can request a specific shampoo, such as oatmeal or tearless, to lather up your pup. Dogs are dried both by hand and with a forced-air dryer. Prices vary depending on the size of your dog and its grooming needs.

## Peaches & Gable

(610) 688-0057
Lancaster County Farmers Market
389 W Lancaster Ave
(@ Eagle Rd)
Wayne, PA 19087
**Hours:** Wed – Sat 7 AM – 4 PM
**Payment:** Checks
**Price Range:** $$$

Tucked between flower and food vendors in the narrow aisles of the Farmers Market, this tiny booth offers up treats and plenty of goods for those wanting to spoil the dog in their life. Edible offerings include wheat-free as well as bacon-and-cheese and peanut-butter-flavored biscuits. The lamb jerky is also quite popular. And everything's organic. Food and water dishes range from hand-painted ceramic to stylish stainless steel with breed-specific silhouettes, set in wrought-iron holders. There's a limited selection of toys but they're sort of beside the point here.

## Perfect Pooch

(610) 337-7698
385 S Gulph Rd
(@ W Church Rd)
King of Prussia, PA 19406
www.perfect-pooch.com
**Hours:** By Appt
**Payment:** Credit Cards
**Price Range:** $$$

Perfect Pooch is ideal for the working professional. Drop your wayward dog off for a seven- to ten-day intensive training program ($600), and a week later pick up your well-trained pup. Trainers are big on positive reinforcement, but you don't have to worry about your dog coming home fat; there are no food rewards at this bow-wow boot camp. In fact, it's BYO food. After your dog completes his training, you must return to the center four times over a four-week period so trainers can work with you and your pup together and make sure he's retaining his education. Dogs must be current on vaccinations to be admitted.

## Pet Diner

(215) 643-2024
Gennardi Shopping Center: Welsh Rd
(@ Norristown Rd)
Maple Glen, PA 19002
**Hours:** Mon – Fri 10 AM – 6 PM,
Sat 10 AM – 5 PM
Sun 10 AM – 3 PM
**Payment:** Credit Cards, Checks
**Price Range:** $$

This small pet-supply store sells specialty foods for dogs, cats, and other small animals. The store also features a full line of grooming supplies and dog shampoos, including Tropiclean, which will leave your pup smelling like coconuts. And if you have a purse-sized pup, you've come to the right place; their dog beds are specifically suited for smaller dogs. Take the time to chat with owner/manager Ruth, and at the very least you will come away with a useful tidbit or two.

# Pet Nanny

(610) 825-5441

**Hours:** By Appt
**Payment:** Checks
**Price Range:** $$

With Colleen Parson's Pet Nanny service, no one will know you're away — even your dog might not notice. The Pet Nanny's 22-point checklist includes disarming/setting security systems, watering houseplants, and collecting newspapers and mail. In addition to dog walking, sitters play ball, administer medication, inspect coats, and make sure dogs are eating and drinking. Visits run $15 for two pets; shopping and pet-food delivery is $15 per trip; pet-taxi service is $15 one way (within a set area). With the Bed and Biscuit House Stay, a sitter will sleep over with your pup for $65. Serving the Main Line and Chester County.

# Pet Valu

www.petvalu.com

**Hours:** Mon – Sat 9 AM – 9 PM
         Sun 10 AM – 5 PM
**Payment:** Credit Cards, Checks
**Price Range:** $/$$

## Pet Valu: Ardmore

(610) 660-8682
77 E City Line Ave
(@ Stout Rd)
Bala Cynwyd, PA 19004

## Pet Valu: Center Square

(610) 239-8175
1301 Skippack Pike
(@ Dekalb Pike)
Blue Bell, PA 19422

## Pet Valu: Chesterbrook

(610) 254-9101
550 E Lancaster Ave
(off N Randnor Chester Rd)
Radnor, PA 19087

## Pet Valu: Huntingdon Valley
(215) 942-7922
2138 E County Line Rd
(@ Davisville Rd)
Huntingdon Valley, PA 19006

## Pet Valu: Jenkintown
(215) 572-6349
323 Old York Rd
(@ Greenwood Ave)
Jenkintown, PA 19046

## Pet Valu: Norristown
(610) 277-5090
55 W Germantown Pike
(@ Mill Rd)
Norristown, PA 19401

The Costco of pet stores, Pet Valu provides bulk pet supplies warehouse style. Items include fleece jackets, paw protectors, over 100 styles of pet beds, travel carriers and kennels, plus premium and private-label foods, as well as all of the usual pet-care staples. Toys, of all shapes and sizes, from humongous tug toys to itty-bitty squeaky balls, stretch as far as the eye can see. And they also stock user-friendly grooming products, like the all-natural waterless bath. If you don't see what you want, you can browse their in-store catalog for specialty items. The staff is consistently friendly and knowledgeable.

## Petagree
(610) 353-9799
6 Reese Ave
(between Bishop Hollow Rd & Mary Jane Ln)
Newtown Square, PA 19073
**Hours:** Mon – Fri 7:15 AM – 3 PM
**Payment:** Checks
**Price Range:** $

Getting your pup in for a trim at Petagree around the holidays is tougher than getting into Alison at Blue Bell on a Friday night. They usually only have room for regulars unless it's a small dog with few needs. Pets must be dropped off between 7:15 and 9:30 AM and can be picked up at 1 or 3 PM. They won't hold your pup after 3 PM, so make arrangements.

## PetCare Group

(610) 738-8733
www.petcaregroup.com
**Hours:** By Appt
**Payment:** Checks
**Price Range:** $$

Boasting references from dozens of dogs, all posted prominently on the Web site, PetCare's two-for-one discounts make them a great value for multiple-pet households. A nominal surcharge applies for each additional pet, as well as for last-minute and holiday visits. Standard visits are $15. An hour of playtime in the park is $35; taxi service is $15 one way. PetCare will also administer medications, is happy to stay overnight in your home ($65), and will perform additional household tasks upon request. Insured, bonded, and a member of PSI, PetCare serves Chester County as well as Newton Square and Edgemont in Delaware County.

## Petco

www.petco.com
**Payment:** Credit Cards, Checks
**Price Range:** $/$$/$$$

## Petco: Ardmore

(610) 658-9710
270 E Lancaster Ave
between Indian Creek Rd & Indian Creek Ln
Wynnewood, PA 19096
**Hours:** Mon – Sat 8 AM – 10 PM
　　　　Sun 10 AM – 7 PM

## Petco: Clifton Heights
(610) 259-2448
520 W Baltimore Pike
(between N Bishop & N Oak Aves)
Clifton Heights, PA  19018
**Hours:** Mon – Sat 9 AM – 10 PM
       Sun 10 AM – 8 PM

## Petco: King of Prussia
(610) 337-4484
145 W Dekalb Pike
(between Town Center & N Henderson Rds)
King Of Prussia, PA  19406
**Hours:** Mon – Sun 9 AM – 10 PM

## Petco: Malvern
(610) 644-9959
181 Lancaster Ave
(between Malin & Conestoga Rds)
Malvern, PA  19355
**Hours:** Mon – Sat 9 AM – 9 PM
       Sun 10 AM – 8 PM

## Petco: Montgomeryville
(215) 393-5760
753 Rte 309
(between Vilsmeier & N Wales Rds)
Montgomeryville, PA  18936
**Hours:** Mon – Sat 9 AM – 9 PM
       Sun 10 AM – 8 PM

## Petco: Trappe
(610) 489-9830
130 W Main St
(between 1st & 3rd Aves)
Trappe, PA  19426
**Hours:** Mon – Sat 9 AM – 9 PM
Sun 10 AM – 7 PM

## Petco: Willow Grove
(215) 659-9916
39 York Rd
(between Cherry & Church Sts)
Willow Grove, PA  19090
**Hours:** Mon – Sat 9 AM – 9 PM
Sun 10 AM – 8 PM

For one-stop shopping it's hard to beat the convenience and value of this superstore with locations all over the country. Petco makes it their mission to provide customers with the food, supplements and products they want for their animals. Their bed selection runs the gamut, from orthopedic mattresses, along with sheets and throws, to chaises that would do an interior decorator proud. Get a P.A.L.S. (Petco Animal Lovers Save) card to take advantage of discounts; you may also want to check out their Top Dog program, which offers even greater saving to their most loyal customers. Check the listing for each store's hours and specific service offerings.

## PetSmart
www.petsmart.com
**Payment:** Credit Cards, Checks
**Price Range:** $/$$/$$$

## PetSmart: Broomall
(610) 353-4466
2940 Springfield Rd
(between W Chester Pk & Latches Ln)
Broomall, PA  19008
**Hours:** Mon – Sat 9 AM – 9 PM, Sun 10 AM – 6 PM

## PetSmart: Devon
(610) 644-3676
176 Swedesford Rd
(between Contention Ln & Valley Forge Rd)
Devon, PA  19333
**Hours:** Mon – Sat 9 AM – 9 PM
        Sun 10 AM – 6 PM

## PetSmart: Exton
(610) 518-0250
1010 E Lancaster Rd
(between Woodbine Rd & Country Club Dr)
Downington, PA  19335
**Hours:** Mon – Sat 9 AM – 9 PM
        Sun 10 AM – 6 PM

## PetSmart: Jenkintown
(215) 885-3635
901 Old York Rd
(between Cherry St & Homestead Rd)
Jenkintown, PA  19046
**Hours:** Mon – Sat 9 AM – 9 PM
        Sun 10 AM – 6 PM

## PetSmart: North Wales
(215) 699-9366
145 Witchwood Dr
(between Knapp & Stump Rds)
North Wales, PA  19454
**Hours:** Mon – Sat 9 AM – 9 PM
        Sun 10 AM – 6 PM

## PetSmart: Plymouth Meeting

(610) 567-2933
2100 Chemical Rd (east of I-476)
Plymouth Meeting, PA 19462
**Hours:** Mon – Sat 9 AM – 9 PM
　　　　 Sun 10 AM – 6 PM

This standout superstore is to pet owners what Home Depot is to homeowners. PetSmart stocks an unbelievably wide range of products that will meet almost any budget. They carry the better dog food brands — including Bil-Jac. And whenever possible, they offer all-natural options in their selection of treats, supplements, and skin products. A viewing window allows see-for-yourself grooming so you don't have to worry about what happens behind closed doors. They get major points for promoting their adoptions all the time. And they have a staff that's always available to advise you and to help you find what you need. It's places like PetSmart that give superstores a good name. Check the listing for ech store's hours and specific service offerings.

## Philadelphia Dog Training Club, Inc.

(610)853-9601
Friends School Haverford
851 Buck Ln, (between Walnut Ln & Panmure Rd)
Haverford, PA 19041
www.philadogtraining.org
**Hours:** Tue – Thu 6:30 PM – 9:30 PM
**Payment:** Credit Cards, Checks
**Price Range:** $

Your child might not attend the Friends School Haverford, but there's no reason your pup can't learn a thing or two in their gym. The nonprofit Philadelphia Dog Training Club holds weekly dog- and puppy-training classes here. In addition to being an AKC obedience trials judge, Barbara Doering, PDTC's director and instructor, has more certifications (albeit in dog training) than a doctor. She teaches beginner through advanced classes. Courses (starting at $120) are eight weeks long. Private lessons (designed around your dog's particular issues) are also available ($90 for 90 minutes). Plan ahead, her classes usually fill up at least a month in advance.

## Pickett, Kim

(610) 363-1452
www.kpickett.com
**Hours:** By Appt
**Payment:** Checks
**Price Range:** $$$

As an intuitive healer, Kim Pickett utilizes several alternative
practices, including energy and body work, as well as animal
communication in her unique brand of animal therapy. She
works to strengthen pet/owner relationships, ideally during
sessions in which both parties are present. She addresses such
issues as behavioral problems, chronic pain and disease, and
death and bereavement (for both people and pets). Kim also
does a great deal of work with abused and neglected animals
who are having trouble acclimating to their new homes. An
hour of therapy with you and your pup will run you $80, but if
that's too steep, Kim also offers group workshops.

## Prince's Automotive Repairs & Pet Goodies

(610) 328-3433
N State Rd & N Rolling Rd
Springfield, PA  19064
**Hours:** Mon – Fri 9 AM – 7 PM
     Sat 9 AM – 5 PM
**Payment:** Credit Cards
**Price Range:** $$

This innovative shop allows you to consolidate your errands
— while having your car tuned, browse through the aisles,
and pick up some treats for your pup! Although their products
are mainstream — you won't find organic food or pup-sized
life-jackets here — they have a diverse selection of commercial
foods, pet beds, toys, and products for cats, birds, and fish as
well. And you can pick up a bandanna for your pup on the
way out.

## Radnor Multi-Purpose Trail

Conestoga Rd
(@ Brookside Ave)
Wayne, PA  19087

**Hours:** Every Day: Sunrise to Sunset
**Payment:** Free

Once a railroad bed for the P&W Line, this 50-foot wide 2.2-mile trail runs from Radnor-Chester to Old Sugartown Road. On a sunny day, you'll find well-behaved dogs happily sharing the trail with outdoorsy types, bikers, and joggers, all of whom enjoy the winding stroll under the forest canopy. Leashes are required and pooper-scooper rules are actively enforced, so be sure to pick up after your pup. (You'll find plenty of waste receptacles along the way.)

## Ruff Cuts

(610) 630-1121
2424 W Ridge Pike
(@ Trooper Rd)
Jeffersonville, PA 19403
www.ruffcutsbydonald.com
**Hours:** Mon – Fri 6:30 AM – 7 PM
**Payment:** Credit Cards, Checks
**Price Range:** $

Donald's passion for art, people, and pets led him to a midlife revelation in which he found his inner groomer. He strives to give pups a cut that suits their lifestyle ($55 for a medium-sized dog). Dogs are cage dried with no-heat dryers. Ruff Cuts also offers day care — dogs are provided with toys, bakery-fresh treats, and crates for napping. Typical crowds range from eight to 12 dogs. If your dog is in need of schooling, you can check out the training-daycare combo package (five days will run you $500). Donald's not just for dogs. He also offers his scissoring and styling services to cats, ferrets, and birds. Check the Web site for coupons.

## Spot's — The Place for Paws

(610) 668-SPOT
854 1/2 Montgomery Ave
(@ Iona Ave)
Narberth, PA 19072
**Hours:** Tue – Sat 10 AM – 5 PM
**Payment:** Credit Cards
**Price Range:** $$$

This quaint Narberth shop features contemporary accouterments for discerning dogs and their owners. Pet beds are custom-made — you pick the fabric and size — while off-the-rack items like life jackets, seat belts and backpacks give the pawed set plenty of safety and sartorial options. Poop-freeze (to facilitate waste pickup), feeding bowls, and assorted toys sit alongside health foods and gourmet treats designed to make your dog salivate. The shop's entrance is on Iona Ave.

# Superior Pet
(610) 789-8543
234 Darby Rd
(@ West Chester Pike)
Havertown, PA 19803
www.superiorpet.net
**Hours:** Tue 10 AM – 5 PM
          Wed – Fri 10 AM – 7 PM
          Sat 10 AM – 3 PM
**Payment:** Credit Cards
**Price Range:** $$
Carrying only premium, natural products, Superior Pet is the place to go for all your pet's organic, holistic, alternatively for-mulated, whole grain, and hormone-free needs. From Eagle Pack Holistic Select to California Natural to Innova, this store's wide range of the healthier brands will accommodate most budgets. For years, Superior Pets has helped pups slim down and kept them healthy with supplements and healthy alternatives to low-grade commercial diets. They also carry a full line of natural treats and grooming products, as well as a variety of handmade toys and attractive accessories. Something you want but don't see? The staff will be more than happy to order it for you.

# TMC Dog Waste Disposal Service
**Hours:** By Appt
**Payment:** Credit Cards, Checks
**Price Range:** $$
With weekly backyard cleanings and tools sterilized after every use, TMC Dog Waste Removal scores in Chester, Delaware, and Montgomery counties. TMC charges $12 for weekly service for a one-dog yard and for a two-dog yard is $16. Fees may be higher for more frequent visits, larger yards, and/or multiple dogs. They double bag the waste and will also rake your yard.

# Veterinary Alternatives

(215) 441-5072
**Hours:** By Appt
**Payment:** Checks
**Price Range:** $$$

Liz of Veterinary Alternatives has a degree in human psychology, which explains her understanding of how people's habits can determine the happiness of their pets. During her hour-long home visits, Liz consults owners about household personalities, communication techniques, and environmental influences that may affect their pet's behavior. She has helped many a pet through issues like separation anxiety and excessive barking. Appointments should be made at least two days in advance.

# Bucks County

## ALTERNATIVE PRODUCTS/SERVICES

**Doylestown**
Doylestown Animal Medical Clinic

**Newtown**
Keystone Veterinary Hospital

**Richboro**
Lick Your Chops of Richboro

**Washington Crossing**
Tail Waggers Boutique

**Yardley**
Animal Healing Center

## ANESTHESIA-FREE TEETH CLEANING

**Doylestown**
Doylestown Animal Medical Clinic

**Langhorne**
Bucks County Pet Grooming

## ANIMAL HOSPITALS & VET CLINICS

**Doylestown**
Doylestown Animal Medical Clinic

**New Hope**
New Hope Veterinary Hospital

**Newtown**
Keystone Veterinary Hospital
Sycamore Veterinary Hospital

**Quakertown**
Quakertown Veterinary Clinic

**Richboro**
Animal Hospital of Richboro

**Warrington**
Bucks County Veterinary Emergency Trauma Services

**Washington Crossing**
Washington Crossing Animal Hospital

**Yardley**
Animal Healing Center
Makefield Animal Hospital Inc.

# CAT SERVICES/PRODUCTS AVAILABLE

**All Neighborhoods**
Aunt Ellen's Pet Sitting Service
Happy Hounds and Pampered Pussy Cats
Irish Sitter
Pets Comfort Plus

**Bensalem**
A Touch Of Class Pet Grooming
Petco: Bensalem

**Doylestown**
Accent on Animals: Doylestown
Doylestown Animal Medical Clinic
P&A Pet Foods
Pet Valu: Doylestown

**Dublin**
Dublin Agway

**Fairless Hills**
PetSmart: Fairless Hills

**Feasterville Trevose**
Petco: Feasterville

**Langhorne**
Bucks County Pet Grooming
Trevose Pet Grooming Center

**Levittown**
All God's Creatures
Beth's Mad About Dogs

**Mechanicsville**
Bucks County Pet Care

**New Britain**
Happy Tails Dog Grooming
Pet Pantry

**New Hope**
Jake and Elwood's House of Chews
New Hope Pet Center
New Hope Veterinary Hospital

**Newtown**
Keystone Veterinary Hospital
Pet Valu: Newton
Reigning Dogs & Cats
Sycamore Veterinary Hospital

**Perkasie**
Edwards Pet Supply Store

**Plumsteadville**
Plain & Fancy Grooming Salon

**Quakertown**
Quakertown Veterinary Clinic

**Richboro**
Animal Hospital of Richboro
Animal Inn of Richboro

**Solebury Township**
Grooming Den, The

**Warminster**
A Paw Above Grooming Salon
As the Fur Flies
Petco: Warminster
PetSmart: Warminster

**Warrington**
Bucks County Veterinary Emergency Trauma Services

**Washington Crossing**
Amber Beech Kennels
Tail Waggers Boutique
Washington Crossing Animal Hospital

**Yardley**
Animal Healing Center
Makefield Animal Hospital Inc.

# CITY DOG PICKS

**All Neighborhoods**
Pets Comfort Plus **(S)**

**Bensalem**
All Breed Dog Training

**Chalfont**
Tender Love & Clipper

**Doylestown**
Accent on Animals: Doylestown
P&A Pet Foods

**Dublin**
Dublin Agway

**New Hope**
Bow Wow: A Shop For You And Your Dog
Jake and Elwood's House of Chews
New Hope Pet Center

**Newtown**
Reigning Dogs & Cats

**Perkasie**
Edwards Pet Supply Store

**Richboro**
Lick Your Chops of Richboro

**Upper Black Eddy**
Delaware Canal State Park

# DOG BOARDING

**Mechanicsville**
Bucks County Pet Care

**Newtown**
Keystone Veterinary Hospital

**Quakertown**
Quakertown Veterinary Clinic

**Richboro**
Animal Inn of Richboro

**Solebury Township**
Grooming Den, The

**Upper Makefield**
A Home Away From Home

**Warrington**
Dog District

**Washington Crossing**
Amber Beech Kennels
Washington Crossing Animal Hospital

# DOG DAY CARE

**Quakertown**
Quakertown Veterinary Clinic

**Upper Makefield**
A Home Away From Home

**Warrington**
Dog District

# DOG GROOMING

**All Neighborhoods**
Lucky Dog Mobile Grooming

**Bensalem**
A Touch Of Class Pet Grooming
Canine Design

**Chalfont**
Tender Love & Clipper

**Fairless Hills**
PetSmart: Fairless Hills

**Langhorne**
Bucks County Pet Grooming
Trevose Pet Grooming Center

**Levittown**
All God's Creatures
Beth's Mad About Dogs

**Mechanicsville**
Bucks County Pet Care

**New Britain**
Happy Tails Dog Grooming

**New Hope**
New Hope Pet Center

**Plumsteadville**
Plain & Fancy Grooming Salon

**Quakertown**
Quakertown Veterinary Clinic

**Richboro**
Animal Inn of Richboro

**Solebury Township**
Grooming Den, The

**Warminster**
A Paw Above Grooming Salon

**Warminster**
As the Fur Flies
Petco: Warminster
PetSmart: Warminster

**Warrington**
Dog District

**Washington Crossing**
Amber Beech Kennels

# DOG PARKS & TRAILS

**Upper Black Eddy**
Delaware Canal State Park

# DOG TRAINING

**Bensalem**
All Breed Dog Training

**Fairless Hills**
PetSmart: Fairless Hills

**Jamison**
County Kennels Dog Training

**Penndel**
Canine Academy

# DOG WALKING/PET SITTING
Aunt Ellen's Pet Sitting Service
Happy Hounds and Pampered Pussy Cats
Irish Sitter
Pets Comfort Plus

# LOW-COST VACCINATION CLINICS

**Bensalem**
Petco: Bensalem

**Doylestown**
Doylestown Animal Medical Clnic

**Fairless Hills**
PetSmart: Fairless Hills

**Feasterville Trevose**
Petco: Feasterville

**Warminster**
Petco: Warminster
PetSmart: Warminster

## ON-SITE PET ADOPTIONS

**Fairless Hills**
PetSmart: Fairless Hills

**Feasterville Trevose**
Petco: Feasterville

**Warminster**
Petco: Warminster
PetSmart: Warminster

## PET-SUPPLY STORES

**Bensalem**
Petco: Bensalem

**Doylestown**
Accent on Animals: Doylestown
P&A Pet Foods
Pet Valu: Doylestown

**Dublin**
Dublin Agway

**Fairless Hills**
PetSmart: Fairless Hills

**Feasterville Trevose**
Petco: Feasterville

**New Brittain**
Pet Pantry

**New Hope**
Bow Wow: A Shop For You And Your Dog
Jake and Elwood's House of Chews
New Hope Pet Center

**Newtown**
Pet Valu: Newton
Reigning Dogs & Cats

**Perkasie**
Edwards Pet Supply Store

**Richboro**
Lick Your Chops of Richboro

**Warminster**
Petco: Warminster
PetSmart: Warminster

**Washington Crossing**
Tail Waggers Boutique

# PHOTOGRAPHY/PAINTINGS

**Feasterville Trevose**
Petco: Feasterville

**Warminster**
Petco: Warminster

# POOP-REMOVAL SERVICE

Myers Dog Waste Cleanup

# General Listings

## A Home Away From Home

(215) 598-3951
428 Brownsburg Rd
(near Carousel Village)
Upper Makefield, PA 18940
**Hours:** Mon – Fri 7 AM – 8 PM
Sat 7 AM – 3 PM
**Payment:** Credit Cards, Checks
**Price Range:** $$

Thanks to its stellar reputation, Home Away From Home, where dogs are under 24 hour supervision, stays packed all summer long. For $15 – $25, dogs stay in one of thirty 5 x 15–foot runs and get two walks per day plus free food. There is a surcharge for additional playtime and for medication administration. The house fare is Science Diet, but you're welcome to bring your dog's favorite brand of chow. Squeaky balls and other toys are welcome, but the bed has to stay home. Your dog's full vaccination records, leash, and collar are required before your dog can check in. First-time customers must pay in advance.

## A Paw Above Grooming Salon

(215) 674-3818
197 York Rd
(between County Line Rd & Street Rd)
Warminster, PA 18974
**Hours:** Tue – Fri 8:30 AM – 4:30 PM
Sat 8:30 AM – 5 PM
**Payment:** Checks
**Price Range:** $$

This attractive, full service grooming salon clips and scrubs both dogs and cats in a homey, friendly environment. Adept at both pet and breed-standard cuts, the groomers here take good care of their charges. Pups are first blown dry with a forced-air dryer, and then finished off with an old-fashioned towel dry. Dogs waiting to be picked up hang out in open crates equipped with cooling fans. Appointments are required. Call a few days in advance during the holidays and summer months, otherwise a day's notice will suffice.

## A Touch Of Class Pet Grooming

(215) 245-6344
5819 Bensalem Blvd
(@ New Falls Rd)
Bensalem, PA  19020
**Hours:** Tue – Sat 9 AM – 5 PM
**Payment:** Credit Cards
**Price Range:**  $$$

Want to get rid of doggie dreads or cat mats? Check out this clean, attractive grooming salon, which offers complete bathing and grooming services to dogs of all sizes and breeds as well as cats. Animal lover David Lea, the salon's owner and groomer, will happily transform your chow from an angry tangled mess into to a fluffy puff ball. Dogs are dried with a handheld forced-air dryer. Appointments should be made a few days in advance.

## Accent on Animals: Doylestown

(215) 340-BARK
4365 Swamp Rd
(@ Rte 313)
Doylestown, PA  18901
**Hours:** Mon – Fri 10 AM – 9 PM
       Sat 9:30 AM – 6 PM
       Sun 11 AM – 5 PM
**Payment:** Credit Cards, Checks
**Price Range:**  $$

Think twice before bringing your dog along to this store, as the narrow aisles afford just enough room for one person to peruse the shelves. But what they lack in space, they make up for with scads of goods. Accent on Animals offers everything from commercial-brand dry and canned foods, toys, and dog beds to a great selection of shampoos and vitamins. People offerings include stationery and breed-specific T-shirts. The friendly and helpful staff are obvious animal people. If you're going to the Philadelphia location, bring change for the meters.

## All Breed Dog Training
(215) 271-2888
814 Edgewood Ave
(near Rte 95)
Bensalem, PA 19020
**Hours:** Check Website
**Payment:** Credit Cards
**Price Range:** $$

Building better relationships through mutual understanding is the goal of the six-step training program at Karen Pivitello's All Breed. The basics include a primer in doggie psych. Owner Karen, who has a degree in Animal Science, first teaches you to "read" your dog, then moves on to reward-based positive reinforcement and non-abusive correction training. Private and group sessions are offered for all levels: puppy kindergarten, beginners, advanced beginners, and novices. Should your pup run into trouble between classes, phone sessions are available.

## All God's Creatures
(215) 547-2951
8746 New Falls Rd
(Penn Valley & New Falls Rd)
Levittown, PA 19054
**Hours:** Tue – Sat 8 AM – 5 PM
**Payment:** Credit Cards, Checks
**Price Range:** $$$

This large salon can handle 20 to 30 dogs on a busy day. The four expert groomers are adept at almost all of the breed standard cuts, using hand-scissoring or clippers. However, they do not do hand stripping. Forced-air dryers are used for most of the drying process. However, dogs are cage-dried part of the time. There are several shampoos to choose from, including oatmeal and hypoallergenic. Call for an appointment at least two weeks in advance — 1:30 pm is always the last appointment of the day. Cats welcome.

# Amber Beech Kennels

(215) 493-2201
1040 Taylorsville Rd
(@ 95th St)
Washington Crossing, PA  18977
**Hours:** Mon – Fri 8:30 AM – 6 PM
Sat 8:30 AM – 5 PM
**Payment:** Checks
**Price Range:**  $

With 24/7 supervision from live-in staff and your vet's number speed dialed into their phone, you can rest easy knowing Amber Beech takes the necessary precautions to keep your pup well cared for. Seniors receive special attention at this standout facility that's tops in amenities. Reaching maximum occupancy at 140 dogs, this is not a small place — but all pups receive playtime in the large fenced-in exercise arena. Boarding starts at $20 per day (a surcharge applies for administering meds and late pickups). Grooming is also available — all dogs are dried with no-heat fans. Book one to three months in advance during the holidays and summertime.

# Animal Healing Center

(215) 493-0621
1724 Yardley-Langhorne Rd
(@ Stoney Hill Rd)
Yardley, PA  19067
**Hours:** Mon 9 AM – 5 PM
Tue – Thu 9 AM – 4 PM, 5 PM – 8 PM
Fri 9 AM – 4 PM
Sat 8:15 AM – 1 PM
**Payment:** Credit Cards, Checks
**Price Range:**  $$$

Deva Khalsa and her staff of four veterinarians feel the spiritual is as important as the physical when treating dog ailments. And their many services dovetail Eastern wisdom with Western medicine. Offerings include Bach Flower Essence remedies, massage therapy, canine chiropractic, and allergy relief as well as assistance with a multitude of canine and feline issues. Call for a free consultation. Late hours are available Tuesday, Wednesday, and Thursday.

## Animal Hospital of Richboro

(215) 322-9900
700 2nd St Pike
(@ Street Rd)
Richboro, PA 18954
**Hours:** Mon – Tue 8 AM – 8 PM
Wed 8 AM – 6 PM
Thu 8 AM – 8 PM
Fri 8 AM – 6 PM
Sat 9 AM – 1 PM
**Payment:** Credit Cards, Checks
**Price Range:** $$$
This hospital specializes in keeping dogs and cats comfy
during veterinary procedures with their advanced pain-treat-
ment technology, like morphine patches. Dr. Kramer performs
routine exams ($50), surgeries, spaying/neutering, and other
treatments with the help of four vet techs. Staff members are
friendly, attentive, and work with you to meet your pet's needs.
Same-day appointments can often be accommodated. Beware,
your pup's pain-free bliss will be reflected in your bill.

## Animal Inn of Richboro

(215) 364-2088
700 2nd St Pike
(@ Street Rd)
Richboro, PA 18954
**Hours:** Mon 8:45 AM – 4:30 PM
Tue – Fri 8:30 AM – 4:30 PM
Sat 8:30 AM – 4:15 PM
**Payment:** Credit Cards, Checks, Cash
**Price Range:** $$
Located inside the Animal Hospital of Richboro, this boarding
and grooming facility has been in operation for 12 years.
Animal Inn welcomes cats and dogs of all sizes and breeds.
Grooming includes a bath, haircut, nail trimming, and ear
cleaning. Most animals are dried with a hand dryer, but no-
heat cage dryers are occasionally used. Post-bath, pets hang
out in open, ventilated crates. Boarded dogs stay in 4 x 8–foot
runs, and are walked several times a day. One or two days
notice will usually suffice for boarding; for grooming, schedule
three weeks ahead.

## As the Fur Flies

(215) 442-7474
983 W County Line Rd
(@ Meetinghouse Rd)
Warminster, PA  18974
**Hours:** Mon – Fri 7:30 AM – 5 PM
**Payment:** Credit Cards, Checks
**Price Range:**  $$

When the fur flies at this facility, it's a good thing. Owner
Fred Grout, who's been at this location for seven years, boasts
30 years of hand-scissoring experience, and is adept with
all breeds. Grooming, starting at $35, includes bathing, nail
trimming, ear cleaning, trimming between toe pads, and anal-
gland expression. Dogs are dried with both hand and forced-
air dryers. Brushes and high-quality shampoos are also sold
at the counter of this friendly salon. Schedule appointments a
week or two in advance.

## Aunt Ellen's Pet Sitting Service

(215) 672-4046
**Hours:** Mon – Sun 9 AM – 5 PM
**Payment:** Checks
**Price Range:**  $$

Aunt Ellen, who makes a point of avoiding all contact with
other dogs when she is out and about with your pup, is
nothing if not careful. She's been tending to local dogs, cats,
and rabbits for over two years. She'll make as many visits per
day as you like, give your pup a potty break, bring in the mail,
adjust the blinds, and feed and/or administer medication. Aunt
Ellen makes herself available seven days a week and charges
$15 per visit. The only thing she won't do is stay overnight.

## Beth's Mad About Dogs

(215) 269-2691
167 Fallsington Tullytown Rd
(@ Thornridge Pl)
Levittown, PA  19055
www.bethsmadaboutdogs.com

**Hours:** Tue – Fri 9 AM – 5 PM
Sat 8 AM – 4 PM
**Payment:** Credit Cards, Checks
**Price Range:** $$

Beth's passion for pets is immediately apparent when you step into this adorable salon that prides itself on its old-fashioned customer service and quality work. Beth, who does mostly hand scissoring, has spent the last 20 years honing her craft and can handle just about any cut. Organic flea- and tick-control products are available, along with a variety of shampoos for your dog's delicate tresses, including oatmeal formulations for sensitive skins. Dogs are hand dried with fans that circulate room-temperature air into pets' crates. You can purchase their products to take home, or you can bring your own for them to use. Same- or next-day appointments can often be accommodated.

## Bow Wow: A Shop For You And Your Dog

(215) 862-9871
102C South Main St
(@ Mechanic St)
New Hope, PA 18938
**Hours:** Mon – Fri 10:30 AM – 6 PM
Sat 10 AM – 9 PM
Sun 10:30 AM – 6:30 PM
**Payment:** Credit Cards
**Price Range:** $$$

This chic pup boutique has something for everyone: buy a "Mama's Dog" T-shirt for your arm piece princess or tell the world what you really think of your dog with "The Dog From Hell" T-shirt. Doggles sunglasses, dog hats, and even breed-centric switch plates are tightly stacked in this small but spiffy space. Breed stationery, statuettes, and other novelties are popular, too.

## Bucks County Pet Care

(215) 794-0423
State Hwy 413
(@ Mechanicsville Rd)
Mechanicsville, PA 18934
**Hours:** Mon – Fri 8 AM – 5:30 PM
Sat 8 AM – 5 PM

**Payment:** Checks
**Price Range:** $$
Both cats and dogs are welcome at this fairly large, combination grooming salon/boarding facility. Boarding here is best for pups who like their own space and/or don't play well with others. Each indoor/outdoor kennel is private, but human playtime can be arranged for an additional fee. Pro Plan is the house fare — you are welcome to BYO food but leave the bed at home. If your pup has a lot of fur, she'll be meticulously hand-dried. The cage-dryers are temperature-controlled in the well supervised grooming room.

## Bucks County Pet Grooming

(215) 579-0112
Summit Square Mall
(@ Doublewoods Rd)
Langhorne, PA  19047
**Hours:** Tue – Sat 7:30 AM – 6 PM
**Payment:** Credit Cards, Checks
**Price Range:**  $$
You won't find any hand-scissoring or stripping here. And this salon has been using the same vet-approved neutral-pH shampoo for over 12 years, so if you're looking for the tea-tree-oil shampoo of the hour, Bucks County Grooming most likely isn't for you. However, the salon's loyal following is a testament to their tried-and-true, no-fuss services, which include bathing, clipping, ear cleaning, teeth brushing, and nail trimming. Dogs are cage dried with low-heat, temperature-controlled dryers, under close supervision. Prices start at $25 for small dogs, $35 for large dogs. Appointments can generally be accommodated with one to two days notice.

## Bucks County Veterinary Emergency Trauma Services

(215) 918-2200
978 Easton Rd
(between Bristol & Street Rds)
Warrington, PA  18976
**Hours:** Mon – Thu 6 AM – 8 PM
         **Emergency Services:** Fri 6 PM – Mon 8 PM
**Payment:** Credit Cards, Checks
**Price Range:**  $$

This ER for animals is the place to go when you find yourself with a sick or injured pup in the middle of the night. A medium-sized facility, Bucks County is equipped to handle emergency care and trauma services. Needless to say, this is not the place to come for a routine checkup or minor ailment. They are not really set up for routine care or staffed to handle such appointments, and the $85 fee makes it a little impractical.

# Canine Academy

(215) 757-8193
397 W Lincoln Hwy
(@ Glenview Plaza Rte1)
Penndel, PA 19047
www.canineacademypa.com
**Hours:** By Appt
**Payment:** Checks
**Price Range:** $$

A shared background earning titles in the Schutzhund ring brought together trainers Debbie MacDonald and Shirley Miyahara. The backbone of the Canine Academy's faculty, this duo believes in finding the motivational method that works with your dog's individual personality. Since 1973, this training facility has graduated packs of canine good citizens (CGC), dog agility dynamos and well-mannered family pets. Popular courses include in-home obedience ($210 for three one-hour sessions), group obedience ($120 for six sessions), the CGC prep course ($120 for six sessions), and advanced small-group obedience clinics ($180 for three sessions).

# Canine Design

(215) 639-1160
1550 Bristol Pike
(@ Rte 63)
Bensalem, PA 19020
**Hours:** Mon 12 PM – 6 PM
Tue – Wed 8 AM – 6 PM
Thu – Fri 9 AM – 6 PM
**Payment:** Credit Cards
**Price Range:** $$

This standout salon is run by husband-and-wife team, George and Betty Barth, with all of the expertise that 30 years in the business brings. They offer complete grooming services for all sizes and breeds. A master groomer, George does various kinds of breed-standard cuts ($65 for a standard poodle) but he's just as happy to give your chow a teddy bear cut. Canine Design cage dries dogs with no-heat fans. Breeders of Petite Basset Griffon Vendeens (PBGV), George and Betty were founding members of the PBGV Club of America, and are to thank for the recognition this young breed receives in the United States.

## County Kennels Dog Training

(215) 598-1599
Training Center
1005 Almshouse Rd
(@ Jacksonville Rd)
Jamison, PA 18929
**Hours:** By Appt
**Payment:** Credit Cards, Checks
**Price Range:** $$
A canine behavioral coach for more than 30 years, Sharon Long's obedience classes are designed to control loud and disorderly dogs. The veteran trainer teaches owners praise-based tactics to silence excessive barkers and manage leash pulling, jumping, and other bad habits. Classes have a nose count of up to eight unruly students. Sharon believes that training a dog to mind his manners in her sometimes-chaotic classes will make him better at minding his p's and q's in the real world. The cost of the Basic Obedience course is $175.

## Delaware Canal State Park

(610) 982-5560
11 Lodi Rd
(@ Red Cliff & River rds)
Upper Black Eddy, PA 18972
www.dcnr.state.pa.us
**Hours:** Every Day: Sunrise to Sunset
**Payment:** Free
Meandering from Easton to Bristol, this towpath sports a smooth surface that's idyllic for point-to-point hikes, and is complete with stunning scenery. The park attracts hikers, cyclists, and mountain bikers as well as joggers and dog walkers — and the path is wide enough to accommodate everyone. Leashes are required, and plenty of trash cans make

it easy to comply with state regulations to pick up after your dog. Visit the Web site for details on closings due to inclement weather, flooding and the like. Weather permitting, it's open every day, including holidays, until sunset.

## Dog District

(215) 918-2292
580 Kansas Rd
(between Easton & Street rds)
Warrington, PA  18976
www.dogdistrict.com
**Hours:** Mon – Fri 7 AM – 7 PM
    Sat 8 AM – 5 PM
**Payment:** Credit Cards, Checks
**Price Range:**  $$$

If you're planning a quick getaway, or just need a few hours of alone time, Dog District offers flexible plans for your pooch. Boasting 2,000 square feet of free play space, the District separates little as well as older dogs from the wound-up adolescents and over-exuberant puppies. The District will not only tire out this second set, but also teach them manners. An initial $15 registration fee and assessment is required. Note to those who tend to be a few minutes behind schedule: the District tacks on surcharges for tardy pickups. Demand is high, so appointments are highly recommended. Grooming is also available.

## Doylestown Animal Medical Clinic

(215) 345-7782
800 N Easton Rd
(@ Rte 313)
Doylestown, PA  18901
www.DoylestownAnimalMedicalClinic.com
**Hours:** Mon – Tue 8 AM – 8 PM, Wed 8:15 AM – 5 PM, Thu 8
    AM – 8 PM, Fri 8:15 AM – 8 PM, Sat 8 AM – 12 PM
**Payment:** Credit Cards, Checks
**Price Range:**  $$

Rated Best of Bucks Mont 2004 by *The Intelligencer*, this small-animal hospital has been tending to local pets since 1983. Not only does this team of five vets provide a host of traditional services, but they also do acupuncture in this spacious, spotless facility. Other services include physical examinations for $46, preventative care, nutrition counseling, orthopedics, dentistry, surgery, and microchipping. A pharmacy and comprehensive laboratory are also on-site. Appointments should be made a few days in advance. Emergencies are referred to the Veterinary Specialty and Emergency Center in Warrington.

## Dublin Agway

(215) 249-3556
10 N Rte 313
(@ Rickert Rd)
Dublin, PA  18917
**Hours:** Mon – Thu 8 AM – 7 PM
　　　　Fri 8 AM – 8 PM
　　　　Sat 8 AM – 7 PM, Sun 9 AM – 5 PM
**Payment:** Credit Cards, Checks
**Price Range:**  $$
The heart of this huge farm- and garden-supply store is animal supplies and accessories. They carry one of the area's largest selections of commercial-brand dog foods, as well as specialty lines such as Blue Seal Dog Biscuits ($4.99 for a small bag) and Bark Bars. BioGroom and Tropi-Clean shampoos, an array of brushes, and more grooming tools than you'd ever know what to do with make for pleasant browsing. Don't miss practical lifestyle offerings like pet beds, mesh gates, and radio fences. On the fun side, there are stuffed toys and matching dog-and-person cap/T-shirt combos.

## Edwards Pet Supply Store

(215) 257-7864
1126 Market St
(@ Rich Rd)
Perkasie, PA  18944
**Hours:** Mon – Fri 8 AM – 8 PM, Sat 8 AM – 5 PM
**Payment:** Checks
**Price Range:**  $$
On the outside, Edward's looks more ranch house than pet-supply store. But on the inside, this shop is filled from top to bottom with upscale commercial brands (including ProPlan, Innova, and Science Diet) and treats for dogs and cats. Nutritional supplements include New Pro ($10 for a small

bottle), as well as Wellness and Pet Tab brands. No novelty items or accessories here, just a wide-ranging selection of collars and leashes, pet beds (ranging from $7 to $40) for pups of all sizes, as well as grooming supplies. The manager is a friendly man, eager to assist you with your selection.

# Grooming Den, The
(215) 862-5686
6824 Rte 63
(@ Comfort Rd)
Solebury Township, PA 18963
**Hours:** Tue – Sat 9:30 AM – 5:30 PM
**Payment:** Checks
**Price Range:** $$$

Beth does a booming business without stepping foot outside her front door. Grooming services include hand-scissored cuts, temperature-controlled cage drying, a homey, stress-free atmosphere, and big kennels for waiting dogs. For sleepovers, she can accommodate seven to ten dogs at a time in her two spare bedrooms, where dogs doze in spacious kennels. Be sure to pack a bag for your pup because it's BYO food, toys, and bedding. To enjoy her down-home services, you must pay half your fee up front. And don't be put off if she doesn't answer the phone; leaving a message on her answering machine is standard procedure. Cats are welcome.

# Happy Hounds and Pampered Pussy Cats
(215) 822-1434
**Hours:** By Appt
**Payment:** Checks
**Price Range:** $$

Boasting a degree in small-animal science, vet tech Brenda Bolster has been operating her on-the-side pet-sitting business for the last seven years. Brenda Bolster always schedules a pre-walk consultation so that she can meet your pet and discuss your particular needs. Visits are $15. She will give your dog as much exercise as he needs, administer medication, collect mail, take the trash out, and adjust blinds, all at no extra charge. Service depends on availability. Due to her day job, she requires two weeks advance notice.

# Happy Tails Dog Grooming

(215) 997-8447
309 Hilltown Pike
(Across from Soto's Diner)
New Britain, PA  18901
**Hours:** Mon – Fri 7:30 AM – 6:30 PM
         Alternate weekends 7:30 AM – 6:30 PM
**Payment:** Checks
**Price Range:**  $$

With 12 years in the grooming business, Therese can confidently style any dog that walks through her door. She does mostly hand scissoring, using clippers only when necessary. After a thorough bathing, dogs are dried in ventilated cages with cage dryers that turn off automatically if the temperature inside changes. She does not administer flea treatments of any kind, because she believes they are too toxic. You can generally book an appointment with a few days' notice, but you'll have to leave a message and wait for Therese to call you back. Cats are welcome, but only on Mondays after 5 PM, and Tuesdays and Thursdays from 2 PM until closing.

# Irish Sitter

(215) 493-7459
**Hours:** By Appt
**Payment:** Checks
**Price Range:**  $$

If you're looking for a neighborly type couple to drop in on your dog, call Pat and Ed Monigan. This couple has built a thriving pet-sitting business over the last 13 years. Prices start at $20 a day, with extra fees for medication and multiple daily visits. Services include daily walks, feeding of all house pets, and scooping litter boxes. The Monigans will come to your house for a meet-and-greet consultation to get to know your pet before taking you on as a client.  Serving Yardley, Lower Makefield, Newtown, and Newtown Square.

## Jake and Elwood's House of Chews

(215) 862-2533
122 S Main St
(@ Waterloo St)
New Hope, PA 18938
www.jakeandelwoodshouseofchews.com
**Hours:** Mon – Fri 11 AM – 5 PM
Sat 11 AM – 7 PM
Sun 11 AM – 6 PM
**Payment:** Credit Cards, Checks
**Price Range:** $$

Two rescued puppies — the eponymous Jake and Elwood — were the inspiration for this store, which their adoptive family opened to help fund future dog-rescue efforts. Gourmet all-natural treats, including Fat Murrays ($4), funky painted bowls, leashes, clothing, and pet carriers are just a few of the products you will find at this unusual store. Beds shaped like large animals, such as elephants ($65) and leopards ($80), can be purchased for your pet's sleeping pleasure and life jackets, leashes with built-in umbrellas, and booster seats ($40) are also available. If your pup craves quality alone time, you can get him his own tent or pint-sized sofa for lounging in.

## Keystone Veterinary Hospital

(215) 598-3951
428 Brownsburg Rd
(@ Rte 413)
Newtown, PA 18940
**Hours:** Mon – Fri 7 AM – 5 PM
Sat 7 AM – 3 PM
**Payment:** Credit Cards, Checks
**Price Range:** $

Eastern medicine and holistic remedies have found their way to Keystone, a progressive facility situated on 65 beautiful acres in Bucks County. Specializing in alternative pet medicine, this animal hospital offers acupuncture, home-opathy, and chiropractic procedures. Keystone also provides traditional medicine and 24-hour emergency care. Owner and resident vet Dr. Michael Tierney can usually accommodate next-day appointments, though his travel schedule sometimes prevents it. Boarding is also available (around $16 per day), and includes at least two walks a day. Optional exercise programs include swimming during the warmer months, and high-speed chases in the large outdoor common play area.

## Lick Your Chops of Richboro

(215) 322-5266
700 N 2nd St Pike
(@ Tanyard Rd)
Richboro, PA 18954
**Hours:** Mon – Fri 9:30 AM – 7:30 PM
Sat 9:30 AM – 5 PM
Sun 11 AM – 4 PM
**Payment:** Credit Cards, Checks
**Price Range:** $$

Lick Your Chops is a true Philly original. This upscale retail institution defines four-footed style for Bucks County canines. Their extensive holistic/all-natural pet-food section is headlined by the house brand Lick Your Chops. Pewter leash hooks, ritzy collar charms, and matching leather jackets for you and your pup are just a smattering of the nonfood selections on these inspired shelves. You'll also find pet beds, toys, grooming products, and supplements. The staff consists of avid animal lovers who make owners and dogs alike feel like VIPs.

## Lucky Dog Mobile Grooming

(215) 820-9060
**Hours:** Mon – Sat 8:30 AM – 4 PM
**Payment:** Checks
**Price Range:** $$$

Lucky indeed are the dogs that can avoid the journey to the groomer, and instead get a bath and trim in the comfort of their own driveway. Owner/groomer Ed has provided mobile grooming services for more than 10 years. A dog lover and owner himself, he vows he would never "do anything to your dog that he wouldn't do to his own." He grooms animals in his van, trimming nails, and upon request, administering an all-natural flea bath. All animals are dried with a hand dryer. Appointments should be made at least a week in advance. Prices are high, but much of what you're paying for is the convenience. Serving Doylestown and New Hope.

## Makefield Animal Hospital Inc.

(215) 493-3363
1095 Reading Ave
(@ Yardley Country Club)
Yardley, PA 19067
**Hours:** Mon 9 AM – 11 AM, 4 PM – 6:30 PM
       Tue 3 PM – 5:30 PM
       Wed 4 PM – 6:30 PM
       Fri 9 AM – 11 AM
       Sat 9 AM – 11:30 PM
       **Surgeries:** Tue & Wed Mornings
**Payment:** Credit Cards, Checks
**Price Range:** $$
Headed up by Dr. Franco Marco, this clinic has been serving
the pets of Yardley since the mid '90s. Services include check-
ups ($38), immunizations, basic surgeries, and dental work
under anesthesia. Prescription Diet pet foods are available
on-site, and prescriptions can usually be filled while you wait.
The vet techs will answer routine questions over the phone for
pre-existing clients. Emergencies are referred to the Veterinary
Specialty & Emergency Center across from Neshaminy
High School on Route 1. Book your appointment a week in
advance, as office hours vary by the day and week.

## Myers Dog Waste Cleanup

(215) 258-3977
**Hours:** By Appt
**Payment:** Cash
**Price Range:** $$
Ms. Myers loves dogs so much that she's willing to do the
dirty work of picking up your yard. Not only is scoopin' poop
her specialty, it's all she'll do, so don't ask her to pick up other
kinds of debris. She disposes of the waste in trash cans, so
make sure one is handy. You can book her for a one-time visit
or once a week, depending on your needs. She charges a flat
fee of $50 for the first hour to remove waste from your yard or
lawn. It's best to call at least a few days in advance for
an appointment.

## New Hope Pet Center

(215) 862-2778
12 Village Row
in Logan Square
(@ Rte 202)
New Hope, PA 18938
**Hours:** Mon – Fri 9 AM – 6 PM
  Sat 10 AM – 5 PM,
  Sun 11 AM – 4 PM
**Payment:** Credit Cards, Checks
**Price Range:** $$

This salon garnered its fame under a former name,
Feathered Friends. Now, dogs large and small flock to this
clean, comfortable salon, where a parrot greets you with a
"hiyah" upon entering. Owner/groomer Sue Coeyman will
pamper your pup with a full grooming, including nail
trimming, ear cleaning, bathing, drying, and of course a cut
and/or brushout. Dogs are dried by hand or with a no-heat
cage dryer, under supervision. The retail section offers an
array of grooming tools, accessories, clothes and dog foods,
including Science Diet, Natural Choice, and Wellness. Book
appointments at least a week in advance.

## New Hope Veterinary Hospital

(215) 862-2961
21 N Sugan Rd
(@ Rte 202)
New Hope, PA 18938
**Hours:** Mon – Fri 8:30 AM – 5 PM
  Sat 9 AM – 12 PM
**Payment:** Checks
**Price Range:** $

New Hope makes basic veterinary treatment convenient for
area pets. Services include exams (starting at $42), vaccina-
tions, routine procedures like spaying/neutering (starting at
$190), and surgeries. Appointments can usually be scheduled
within 24 hours. New Hope Veterinary Hospital refers most
emergencies to the Veterinary Specialty & Emergency Center
across the street from Neshaminy High School.

## P&A Pet Foods

(215) 348-3738
826 N Easton Rd
(@ Rte 313)
Doylestown, PA  18901
**Hours:** Mon – Fri 9 AM – 6 PM
Sat 9 AM – 5 PM,
Sun 10 AM – 3 PM
**Payment:** Credit Cards, Checks
**Price Range:**  $$
P&A Pet Foods is one of the best values in Doylestown.
This spacious pet-supply store has a wide array of quality
merchandise, and an on-site bakery. Be warned: the
fresh-baked cakes ($6 for a small one) smell good enough
to pull out of your pup's mouth. Other offerings include
shampoos, Old Mother Hubbard treats and chews, and foods
like Wellness, Pedigree, and Innova. And for the pedigree-
obsessed, there's breed-themed stationary. The staff is friendly
and eager to help with all questions pertaining to their favorite
subject — you guessed it — dogs.

## Pet Pantry

(215) 489-3171
432 Town Center
(@ Rte 202)
New Brittain, PA  18901
**Hours:** Mon – Fri 10:30 AM – 6 PM ·
Sat 10 AM – 4 PM
**Payment:** Credit Cards, Checks
**Price Range:**  $$
Space is a premium at this small pet-supply shop so if you're
shopping for accessories or dog beds, you'll have to wait for
the holidays, when they stock up. The rest of the year, you can
count on the Pet Pantry for healthy foods like Innova ($.99 a
can) and California Natural, as well as foods for dogs with
sensitive stomachs, such as Verus ($1.19 a can), and Greenies
dog treats. Dog shampoos include Bio Groom and Veterinary
Best. The friendly manager is efficient and helpful.

## Pet Valu

www.petvalu.com
**Hours:** Mon – Sat 9 AM – 9 PM
Sun 10 AM – 5 PM
**Payment:** Credit Cards, Checks
**Price Range:** $/$$

## Pet Valu: Doylestown

(215) 489-7810
73 Old Dublin Pike
Mercer Sq Plaza
(@ Main St)
Doylestown, PA  18901

## Pet Valu: Newton

(215) 504-7170
2814 S Eagle Rd
(@ Silo Dr)
Newtown, PA  18940
The Costco of pet stores, Pet Valu provides bulk pet supplies
warehouse style. Items include fleece jackets, paw protectors,
over 100 styles of pet beds, travel carriers and kennels, plus
premium and private-label foods, as well as all of the usual
pet-care staples. Toys, of all shapes and sizes, from humongous
tug toys to itty-bitty squeaky balls, stretch as far as the eye can
see.  And they also stock user-friendly grooming products like
the all-natural waterless bath. If you don't see what you want,
you can browse their in-store catalog for specialty items. The
staff is consistently friendly and knowledgeable.

## Petco

www.petco.com
**Payment:** Credit Cards, Checks
**Price Range:**  $/$$/$$$

## Petco: Bensalem

(215) 245-7133
2355 Saint Rd
(between Knights & Hulmeville Rds)
Bensalem, PA  19020

**Hours:** Mon – Sat 9 AM – 10:30 PM
Sun 9 AM – 8:30 PM

## Petco: Feasterville
(215) 354-0820
97 E Street Road
Bucks County Mall
(between Bustleton Pk & Harding Ave)
Feasterville Trevose, PA 19053
**Hours:** Mon – Sat 9 AM – 10 PM
Sun 10 AM – 8 PM

## Petco: Warminster
(215) 443-5225
624 York Ave
(between W Street & Roberts Rds)
Warminster, PA 18974
**Hours:** Mon – Sat 9 AM – 9 PM
For one-stop shopping it's hard to beat the convenience and
value of this superstore with locations all over the country.
Petco makes it their mission to provide customers with the
food, supplements and products they want for their animals.
Their bed selection runs the gamut, from orthopedic mattresses,
along with sheets and throws, to chaises that would do an
interior decorator proud. Get a P.A.L.S. (Petco Animal Lovers
Save) card to take advantage of discounts; you may also want
to check out their Top Dog program, which offers even greater
saving to their most loyal customers. Check the listing for each
store for hours and specific service offerings.

## Pets Comfort Plus
(215) 538-8886
**Hours:** By Appt
**Payment:** Checks
**Price Range:** $$
Mary Beth Appert, the sole owner/operator of Pets Comfort
Plus, doesn't do sleepovers but she will make up to three
visits a day. This seems to be enough to keep area pups happy,

because after only 18 months she is already plenty popular. Her trick is to stick as close as possible to the dogs' normal schedule. Standard services include watering plants, collecting mail, and leaving notes about her visits. Add-on services include light grocery shopping and picking up/dropping off dry cleaning. Prices start at $15 a visit, plus $3 for each additional animal. Call to schedule a free in-home consultation. She is fully bonded and insured.

## PetSmart
**Payment:** Credit Cards, Checks
**Price Range:** $/$$/$$$
www.petsmart.com

## PetSmart: Fairless Hills
(215) 949-9602
220 Commerce Blvd
(off Oxford Valley Rd, @ N Buckstown Dr)
Fairless Hills, PA 19030
**Hours:** Mon – Sat 9 AM – 9 PM
Sun 10 AM – 6 PM

## PetSmart: Warminster
(215) 773-9016
934 O Street Rd
(between Norristown & York Rds)
Warminster, PA 18974
**Hours:** Mon – Sat 8 AM – 9 PM
Sun 9 AM – 6 PM

This standout superstore is to pet owners what Home Depot is to homeowners. PetSmart stocks an unbelievably wide range of products that will meet almost any budget. They carry the better dog food brands — including Bil-Jac. And whenever possible, they offer all-natural options in their selection of treats, supplements and skin products. A viewing window allows see-for-yourself grooming so you don't have to worry about what happens behind closed doors. They get major points for promoting their adoptions all the time. And they have a staff that's always available to advise you and to help you find what you need. It's places like PetSmart that give superstores a good name. Check the listing for each store's hours and specific service offerings.

## Plain & Fancy Grooming Salon

(215) 766-1399
5876 Easton Rd
(between Stump Rd & Rte 611)
Plumsteadville, PA  18949
www.plain-fancy.com

**Hours:** Mon, Wed, Fri 8 AM – 5 PM, Tue 10:30 AM – 4 PM
Thu 12 PM – 7 PM, Sat 9 AM – 3 PM
**Payment:** Credit Cards, Checks
**Price Range:** $$

Georgia and Lenore, the two owners of this clean, comfortable, grooming facility boast a combined 40-plus years in the business as well as master groomer certifications. Georgia owned the original Plain & Fancy in Ottsville before partnering up with Lenore, who was well known in Reading as a pup-styling perfectionist. These hand-scissoring experts will groom both dogs and cats of all breeds and fur types. Animals are dried most of the way with forced-air hand dryers; however, a box fan is often employed for finishing touches. Grooming starts at $45 for a medium-sized dog. Book at least a week in advance.

## Quakertown Veterinary Clinic

(215) 536-6245
2250 Old Bethlehem Pike
(just past Portzer Rd)
Quakertown, PA  18951
www.quakertownvetclinc.com

**Hours:** Every Day: 24 Hours
**Payment:** Credit Cards, Checks
**Price Range:** $$$

This enormous, state-of-the-art hospital boasts 20 on-staff veterinarians, who tend to dogs, cats, mice, pigs, chickens, rabbits, exotic birds, and horses. Specialties include orthopedics, ophthalmology, and cardiology. Larger animals are treated in the building adjacent to the main facility. Quakertown also offers grooming, day care, and boarding ($17 – $25 per night, depending on the size of your dog's run). Four walks a day and a free bath are standard. The primary emergency facility for Bucks County, Quakertown never closes. (Emergency fees apply, in addition to standard treatment fees.)

# Reigning Dogs & Cats

(215) 497-7477
30 West Rd
(Village @ Newtown Shopping Center)
Newtown, PA  18940
www.reigningdogsandcats.com
**Hours:** Mon – Fri 10 AM – 9 PM, Sat – Sun 10 AM – 6 PM
**Payment:** Credit Cards, Checks
**Price Range:**  $$$

Enter this pup paradise and let your nose, or your pup, lead you to the "The Royal Barkery," where you'll find human-grade treats like Piccolo Puppy Pizzas, Colli-e-Clairs, Italian Greyhound Breadsticks, and Pawberry Paws. You'll also find many of the best dog-food brands here. In addition to traditional canine coats, sports-fan pups can dress the part with Eagles and Flyers jerseys. Beds come in all shapes (cushions, mattresses, sofas, four posters) and sizes (from small enough for a teacup chihuahua to large enough for a Newfoundland). Prices run on the high side but you'll have a tough time finding such a fabulous array of eclectic merchandise anywhere else in the city.

# Sycamore Veterinary Hospital

(215) 968-0509
228 N Sycamore St
(@ Eagle Rd)
Newtown, PA  18940
**Hours:** Mon, Wed 9:30 AM – 8 PM,
         Tue, Fri 9:30 AM – 6 PM, Thu 9:30 AM – 7:30 PM
**Payment:** Credit Cards, Checks
**Price Range:**  $$

Pets and people alike seem to be soothed by the soft music piped into the waiting room at Sycamore Veterinary Hospital. And if the music doesn't do it, the personable staff will put you and your dog instantly at ease. Boasting more than 20 years of experience, Dr. Neubauer and his team make every effort to see that canine and feline patients' needs are met in this well-scrubbed facility. Whenever possible, surgical procedures are performed with a laser to hasten recovery time and minimize pain. Routine appointments should be scheduled a day or two in advance. If it's an emergency, just show up and they will tend to your pet ASAP.

## Tail Waggers Boutique
(215) 493-8284
1240 General Washington Memorial Blvd
(@ Taylorsville Rd)
Washington Crossing, PA  18977
**Hours:** Mon 8:30 AM – 7 PM
Tue – Fri 8:30 AM – 6 PM
Sat 8:30 AM – 12 PM
**Payment:** Credit Cards, Checks
**Price Range:** $$$
Let your dog flop on a memory foam mattress from Tail
Waggers and you'll never find him lounging on cedar chips
again. This boutique makes the dog's life the only life worth
living — with hand-painted porcelain food bowls, embossed
leather collars, and a collection of whimsical dog toys. For the
health conscious, organic, all-natural foods as well as hearty
snacks are front-and-center on these well-stocked aisles. Get
practical with doggie diapers, skunk-odor remover, and
tearless shampoo. Don't miss the cuddly section devoted to
dog clothes — paw through fleece, leather, and hand-knitted
sweaters. Prices are high, but quality is excellent and there is
always something on sale.

## Tender Love & Clipper
(215) 822-6660
47 E Butler Ave
(@ Kearne St)
Chalfont, PA  18914
**Hours:** Tue – Sat 9 AM – 3 PM
**Payment:** Checks
**Price Range:** $$
Specializing in Westies, this boutique salon concentrates on
small to medium-sized dogs. Owner/groomer Lisa, who
graduated from the Pennsylvania School of Dog Grooming and
is a member of the Dog Grooming Association, boasts 19 years
of experience. Among her tricks of the trade are utilizing cage
dryers (under supervision) to start the drying process, and then
finishing with a hand dryer for the perfect fluff. Before and
after their table time, dogs rest in open, well-ventilated cages.
Call at least a week ahead for an appointment.

## Trevose Pet Grooming Center

(215) 357-3477
3959 Brownsville Rd
(@ Hazel Ave)
Langhorne, PA 19053
**Hours:** Tue – Sat 9 AM – 4 PM
**Payment:** Checks
**Price Range:** $$

Boasting 45 years of experience and 40 years in her own shop, the friendly owner of Trevose Grooming gives precise, loving care to Bucks County pets. She uses only all-natural products. Dogs are always hand dried. Nail clipping and ear cleaning can be added on to the bath and cut. She cannot accommodate over-sized dogs and will only work on difficult dogs if they are sedated. Cats are accepted on occasion. Appointments should be made two weeks to a month in advance.

## Washington Crossing Animal Hospital

(215) 493-5986
1240 Rte 532
(a bit past Taylorsville Rd)
Washington Crossing, PA 18977
**Hours:** Mon 8:30 AM – 7 PM
　　　　Tue – Fri 8:30 AM – 6 PM
　　　　Sat 8:30 AM – 12 PM
**Payment:** Credit Cards, Checks
**Price Range:** $$$

This clean, accommodating veterinary office adjoins with Tail Waggers Boutique, giving pets and people a chance to shop while they wait. Two vets care for pets' needs, offering standard procedures, routine surgeries, and dental work. They also employ an ultrasound specialist, who is on call as needed. Anesthesia is used for dental examinations and treatments, during which pets also receive a free pedicure. If your pup needs more specialized care than they are able to provide, they will refer you to another vet. Prices start at $42 for a routine checkup. Appointments are usually booked at least a week out.

# Camden, Trenton & Surrounding

## ALTERNATIVE PRODUCTS/SERVICES

**Trenton**
Reigning Dogs and Cats Grooming and Massage
Debbie's Pampered Pets

**Princeton**
Hazel & Hannah's Pawtisserie

## ANESTHESIA-FREE TEETH CLEANING

**Pennington**
Pennington Veterinary Clinic at Pennytown

**Trenton**
Nottingham Animal Hospital
Reigning Dogs and Cats Grooming and Massage

## ANIMAL HOSPITALS & VET CLINICS

**Hopewell**
Hopewell Veterinary Group

**Lambertville**
Lambertville Animal Clinic

**Pennington**
Pennington Veterinary Clinic at Pennytown

**Princeton**
Lawrence Animal Hospital
Princeton Animal Hospital

**Trenton**
Chesterfield Veterinary Clinic
Ewing Veterinary Hospital
Hamilton Veterinary Clinic
Nottingham Animal Hospital
Quaker Bridge Animal Hospital
Trenton Veterinary Hospital
Veterinary Care Center

**West Trenton**
West Trenton Animal Hospital

**West Windsor**
Edinburg Animal Hospital

## CAT SERVICES/PRODUCTS AVAILABLE

**Burlington**
Precious Pets: Burlington

**Cherry Hill**
Pet Valu: Cherry Hill
Petco: Cherry Hill
PetSmart: Cherry Hill

**Cinnaminson**
Petco: Cinnaminson

**Deptford**
Petco: Deptford
PetSmart: Deptford

**Hightstown**
Precious Pets: Hightstown

**Hopewell**
Hopewell Veterinary Group Inc.

**Lambertville**
Lambertville Animal Clinic

**Laurel Springs**
Pet Valu: Laurel Springs

**Lawrence**
Lawrence Animal Hospital

**Marlton**
Pet Valu: Marlton

**Moorsetown**
PetSmart: Moorestown

**Pennington**
Pennington Veterinary Clinic at Pennytown
Rosedale Mills

**Pennsauken**
Petco: Pennsauken

**Princeton**
Hazel & Hannah's Pawtisserie
Petco: Princeton

PetSmart: Princeton
Princeton Animal Hospital

**Sewell**
Pet Valu: Sewell

**Sicklerville**
Pet Valu: Sicklerville

**Trenton**
Chesterfield Veterinary Clinic
Debbie's Pampered Pets
Ewing Veterinary Hospital
Hamilton Veterinary Clinic
Paws Pet Grooming & Supplies
Precious Pets: Trenton
Quaker Bridge Animal Hospital
Reigning Dogs and Cats Grooming and Massage
Trenton Veterinary Hospital
Veterinary Care Center
Whiskers & Tails

**West Trenton**
West Trenton Animal Hospital

**West Windsor**
Edinburg Animal Hospital

**Willingboro**
Petco: Willingboro

# CITY DOG PICKS

**Princeton**
Hazel & Hannah's Pawtisserie

**Trenton**
Golden Grange Kennels

# DOG BOARDING

**Cherry Hill**
All Good Dogs Daycare, Inc.: Cherry Hill

**Cinnaminson**
Best Friends: Cinnaminson

**Hopewell**
Hopewell Valley Kennel

**Lambertville**
Pierson Creek Kennels **(S)**

**Lawrenceville**
Curry Corner, The **(S)**

**Monmouth Junction**
All Good Dogs Daycare, Inc.: Monmouth Junction

**Princeton**
Behrwood Pet Motel
Weber's Boarding and Training

**Trenton**
Chesterfield Kennels Dog Boarding
Golden Grange Kennels

**West Berlin**
Best Friends: West Berlin

# DOG DAY CARE

**Cherry Hill**
All Good Dogs Daycare, Inc.: Cherry Hill

**Cinnaminson**
Best Friends: Cinnaminson

**Hopewell**
Hopewell Valley Kennel

**Lawrenceville**
Curry Corner, The **(S)**

**Marlton**
Dog Days

**Monmouth Junction**
All Good Dogs Daycare, Inc.: Monmouth Junction

**Princeton**
Behrwood Pet Motel
Weber's Boarding and Training

**Trenton**
Chesterfield Kennels Dog Boarding

**West Berlin**
Best Friends: West Berlin

# DOG GROOMING

**Cherry Hill**
All Good Dogs Daycare, Inc.: Cherry Hill
Petco: Cherry Hill
PetSmart: Cherry Hill

**Cinnaminson**
Best Friends: Cinnaminson
Petco: Cinnaminson

**Deptford**
Petco: Deptford
PetSmart: Deptford

**Lambertville**
Pierson Creek Kennels **(S)**

**Lawrenceville**
Curry Corner, The **(S)**

**Monmouth Junction**
All Good Dogs Daycare, Inc.: Monmouth Junction

**Moorestown**
PetSmart: Moorestown

**Pennington**
Rosedale Mills

**Pennsauken**
Petco: Pennsauken

**Princeton**
Petco: Princeton
PetSmart: Princeton

**Trenton**
Debbie's Pampered Pets **(S)**
Golden Grange Kennels
Paws Pet Grooming & Supplies
Reigning Dogs and Cats Grooming and Massage
Whiskers & Tails

**West Berlin**
Best Friends: West Berlin

# DOG PARKS & TRAILS

**Camden**
Cooper River Park

**Plainsboro**
Plainsboro Township Dog Park

## DOG TRAINING

**Cherry Hill**
PetSmart: Cherry Hill

**Deptford**
PetSmart: Deptford

**Marlton**
Dog Days

**Moorestown**
PetSmart: Moorestown

**Pennington**
Puppergarten

**Princeton**
Weber's Boarding and Training

**Trenton**
Golden Grange Kennels

## LOW-COST VACCINATION CLINICS

**Cherry Hill**
PetSmart: Cherry Hill

**Cinnaminson**
Petco: Cinnaminson

**Deptford**
Petco: Deptford

**Moorestown**
PetSmart: Moorestown

**Pennsauken**
Petco: Pennsauken

**Princeton**
Petco: Princeton
PetSmart: Princeton

**Willingboro**
Petco: Willingboro

## ON-SITE PET ADOPTIONS

**Cherry Hill**
PetSmart: Cherry Hill

**Cinnaminson**
Petco: Cinnaminson

**Deptford**
Petco: Deptford
PetSmart: Deptford

**Moorestown**
PetSmart: Moorestown

**Pennsauken**
Petco: Pennsauken

**Princeton**
Petco: Princeton
PetSmart: Princeton

**Trenton**
Chesterfield Veterinary Clinic

**Willingboro**
Petco: Willingboro

## PET-SUPPLY STORES

**Burlington**
Precious Pets: Burlington

**Cherry Hill**
Pet Valu: Cherry Hill
Petco: Cherry Hill
PetSmart: Cherry Hill

**Cinnaminson**
Petco: Cinnaminson

**Deptford**
Petco: Deptford
PetSmart: Deptford

**Hightstown**
Precious Pets: Hightstown

**Laurel Springs**
Pet Valu: Laurel Springs

**Lawrenceville**
Curry Corner, The **(S)**

**Magnolia**
K-9 Kare Korner

**Marlton**
Pet Valu: Marlton

**Moorestown**
PetSmart: Moorestown

**Pennington**
Rosedale Mills

**Pennsauken**
Petco: Pennsauken

**Princeton**
Hazel & Hannah's Pawtisserie
Petco: Princeton
PetSmart: Princeton

**Sewell**
Pet Valu: Sewell

**Sicklerville**
Pet Valu: Sicklerville

**Trenton**
Precious Pets: Trenton
Reigning Dogs and Cats Grooming and Massage

**Willingboro**
Petco: Willingboro

# PHOTOGRAPHY/PAINTINGS

**All Neighborhoods**
Candid Canine
Joanna's Pet Portraits

**Cherry Hill**
Petco: Cherry Hill

**Deptford**
Petco: Deptford

**Willingboro**
Petco: Willingboro

# SELF-SERVE DOG GROOMING

**Cherry Hill**
Petco: Cherry Hill

# General Listings

## All Good Dogs Daycare, Inc.
www.allgooddogsdaycare.com
**Hours:** Mon – Fri 7 AM – 7 PM
  Sat – Sun 9 AM – 10 PM
**Payment:** Checks
**Price Range:** $$$

## All Good Dogs Daycare, Inc.: Cherry Hill
(609) 275-7177
2306 Church Rd
(between Woods Rd & Chestnut St)
Cherry Hill, NJ  08002

## All Good Dogs Daycare, Inc.: Monmouth Junction
(609) 275-7177
113 Schalks Station Rd
(N of Perrine Rd)
Monmouth Junction, NJ  08852

All Good Dogs Daycare offers an endless list of services to keep your pup busy while you are away. Older dogs are well catered to, with orthopedic mattresses and a separate play area. Boarding accommodations include Winnie the Pooh — and Scooby Doo  — themed suites. The spa offers pampering "pawdicures" and baths — natural, oatmeal, and hypoaller-genic shampoos are standard. All dogs are dried by hand. Day rates are $35 for dogs less than 40 pounds; $40 for dogs over 40 pounds. Boarding is $50 for 24 hours. In addition to round-the-clock TLC, perks at this standout facility that's been featured in The New York Times include holiday treats and birthday cakes. Interview required.

## Behrwood Pet Motel
(609) 452-9077
3402 US Highway 1
(off Rte 1)
Princeton, NJ  08540

**Hours:** Mon – Fri 8:30 AM – 5:30 PM
      Sat 8:30 AM – 3:30 PM
      Sun 4 AM – 5:30 PM
      **Facility Tours:** Tue – Sat 11 AM – 3 PM
**Payment:** Checks
**Price Range:** $

If you forget to bring your pup's bed, he'll be sleeping on paper at Behrwood Pet Motel, but for $15 a night, no one's complaining. The bare-bones kennels come in several sizes. Indoor/outdoor runs are covered with awnings. Depending on the number of guests, up to seven staff members fetch food and water for visiting pups. Bringing your own food and/or medication costs a dollar per serving. Playtime can be purchased in half-hour increments for $5 — social dogs are allowed to play together. The owner lives on-site and provides 24/7 supervision. Potential clients can tour the facility from 11 AM to 3 PM, Tuesdays through Saturdays, to get a feel for the Pet Motel's no-frills offerings.

## Best Friends Pet Resort
www.bestfriendspetcare.com
**Payment:** Credit Cards, Checks
**Price Range:** $$

## Best Friends Pet Resort: Cinnaminson
(856) 661-0707
2500 Rte 73
(@ O'Donnells Ln)
Cinnaminson, NJ 08077
**Hours:** Mon – Fri 8 AM – 6 PM
      Sat 8 AM – 5 PM
      Sun 3 AM – 6 PM

## Best Friends Pet Resort: West Berlin
(856) 719-0888
585 Rte 73
(@ Katherine Ave)
West Berlin, NJ 08091
**Hours:** Mon – Fri 7 AM – 6 PM, Sat 8 AM – 5 PM
      Sun 3 PM – 6 PM

Employees are helpful and knowledgeable at this popular chain, which offers a full range of services. Prices for day care ($15) and boarding ($24 to $30) are quite reasonable, but beware of extras, like playtime and meds, that can drive the fees way up over an extended stay. They offer grooming amenities, including manicures and moisturizing treatments. Forced-air hand dryers and no-heat cage dryers are used. Be sure to ask about the Shedicure — a treatment that combines the FURminator and a carding process; it can reduce shedding up to 80 percent.

## Candid Canine

(800) 43-CANDID
www.candidcanine.com
**Hours:** By Appt
**Payment:** Credit Cards
**Price Range:** $$$

If you think your pup's close-up ready, you may want to call Andrew of Candid Canines, whose portfolio includes dogs basking on beds of roses and pups made-up to look like Broadway divas. Andrew supplies all props, wigs, and costumes. Candid Canine will also capture your pup in action. Or if you want to share the spotlight with your pup, he'll photograph the two of you together. Andrew shoots in color. In addition to the usual photos, Candid Canine also offers prints with a watercolor effect or screened onto stretched canvas. The basic sitting fee is $350; prints are additional. Since he is based in central New Jersey, a travel fee sometimes applies.

## Chesterfield Kennels Dog Boarding

(609) 723-4323
713 Monmouth St
(@ Rte 543)
Trenton, NJ 08609
**Hours:** By Appt
**Payment:** Checks
**Price Range:** $

Playtime, medication, and food are included in Chesterfield's low rates of $18 to $20 per dog. This small, quiet facility houses 14 runs and a 6 x 6-foot fenced-in play area. Dogs are taken out four times a day. Your dog's toys, food, and blanket are welcome, but leave the dog bed at home. With air conditioning in the kennels, it's no surprise their facility books up during the summertime. Howlers are not welcome. Pickup and drop-off are by appointment.

# Chesterfield Veterinary Clinic

(609) 298-3888
8 Newbold Ln
(@ Chesterfield-Georgetown Rd)
Trenton, NJ 08620
www.chesterfieldvetclinic.com
**Hours:** Mon – Tue, Thu 9 AM – 8 PM
Wed, Fri 9 AM – 3 PM
Sat 9 AM – 12 PM
**Payment:** Credit Cards, Checks
**Price Range:** $$

Tucked into a white clapboard cottage, Chesterfield Veterinary Clinic is as homey as a vet's office can be. This thriving practice, which is owned and operated by Rebecca Bonchec, DVM, also includes veterinarians Cynthia Smith and Crystal Murray. Cutting-edge pain treatments, exceptional geriatric and preventative care as well as dental services, all at reasonable prices, make this practice a great option for those seeking a new family veterinarian. Emergencies are referred to one of the eight clinics in Langhorne, Philadelphia, or New Jersey. Appointments can be scheduled within a week. The practice also runs a pet-adoption service.

# Cooper River Park

(856) 225-5431
between N Park & S Park Drs
(between Rte 130 & Grove St)
Camden, NJ 08102
www.co.camden.nj.us/government/offices/parks/pk_cooper.html
**Hours:** Every Day: Sunrise to Sunset
**Payment:** Free

Dogs and people alike love the large dog area at Cooper River Park in Camden. Best-known for its rowing events, this 340-acre park boasts kiddie play areas, softball fields, volleyball courts, numerous places to picnic, and a really impressive sculpture garden. Separate areas are designated for big and small dogs. Amenities include poop bags, water, and adequate lighting. The tricky part is finding pooch paradise: From Route 70 in Pennsauken, take the Cuthbert Boulevard South jughandle. Turn onto North Park Drive behind the Hilton Hotel. North Park Drive ends at the parking lot for the dog park.

## Curry Corner, The

(609) 896-0778
23 Phillips Ave
(@ George St)
Lawrenceville, NJ  08648
www.njcurrycorner.com
**Hours:** Mon – Fri 8:30 AM till the job is done.
**Payment:** Checks
**Price Range:**  $$

Over the last 32 years, The Curry Corner has gathered a devoted following in the Lawrenceville area. The husband-and-wife team that own this facility breed champion Great Danes so it should come as no surprise that short-haired and extra-large dogs are the salon's specialty. Grooming options also include full comb-outs and/or hand scissoring, starting at $50. Dogs are dried with fans and no-heat dryers. Abady, Oxyfresh, and Royal Canine supplements and foods are sold here, as are a selection of hard-to-find grooming products. Day care ($40) and home-style boarding ($30) are offered to established clients. Schedule appointments at least a week in advance during the holiday season.

## Debbie's Pampered Pets

(609) 396-6768
1114 North Olden Ave
(@ Brunswick Ave)
Trenton, NJ  08638
**Hours:** Tue – Sat 7 AM – 3 PM
**Payment:** Checks
**Price Range:**  $$

Debbie is the owner/operator of this salon and given the name, it should come as no surprise that pampering pets is what she loves to do. Standard grooming for a medium-sized dog starts at $47; if you're looking for a breed-standard cut, the price is slightly heftier ($60 – $100). Standard service includes a bath, trim, nail clipping, and ear cleaning. Debbie uses organic products, including the popular oatmeal shampoo or aloe vera conditioner. All drying is done with handheld low-temperature dryers. Appointments can usually be scheduled within a week.

# Dog Days

(856) 985-7086
19 North Maple Ave
(@ Rte 70)
Marlton, NJ  08053
www.dogdaysinc.net
**Hours:** Mon – Fri 6:30 AM – 6:30 PM
**Payment:** Credit Cards
**Price Range:**  $$
This dog day care provides pups with 6,000 square feet for
fun, socialization, and exercise. Small dogs have a separate
playroom, apart from the medium and large dogs. But all the
playrooms have toys, playground equipment, a constant supply
of fresh water, and soft rubber flooring. Pups are given three
to four bathroom breaks a day, in an outside, fenced-in run.
Your pup will be constantly supervised, with at least one staff
member for every 10 to 15 dogs. The day rate is $26. Discount
packages, which never expire, are also available. Dog Days
also offers training and dog birthday parties.

# Edinburg Animal Hospital

(609) 443-1212
1676 Old Trenton Rd
(W of Robinsville Rd)
West Windsor, NJ  08550
www.edinburgvet.com
**Hours:** Mon – Fri 7 AM – 8 PM
          Sat 7 AM – 12 PM
**Payment:** Credit Cards, Checks
**Price Range:**  $$
Don't let the cozy fireplace in the lobby fool you — this
homey hospital belies its New England cottage setting with the
latest technology. Ultrasound and X-ray equipment, radiology
as well as a full tissue lab are tucked into what were once the
bedrooms of this West Windsor home. In addition to routine
exams ($54), vaccinations, and microchipping, Edinburg's
three experienced veterinarians, stay plenty busy with dental
care and surgeries. All appointments should be scheduled
one to three days in advance. Emergencies are referred to the
Veterinary Emergency Center in Langhorne, Pennsylvania.
Discount coupons are available on their Web site.

# Ewing Veterinary Hospital
(609) 882-8090
38 Scotch Rd
(@ Parkway Ave)
Trenton, NJ 08628
**Hours:** Mon – Fri 9 AM – 6 PM
        Sat 9 AM – 12 PM
**Payment:** Checks, Credit Cards
**Price Range:** $
Affordable services and a friendly staff make this hospital a
wise choice for family pet care. Clinic owner and practicing
vet James Nelson, DVM, strives to meet the needs of pets and
their owners. Elective surgery needs to be scheduled at least
a month in advance. Routine visits and checkups ($40) can
usually be scheduled within a week. Dental services under
anesthesia are also available. Prescription Diet pet foods are
available at the front desk. After-hours emergencies are referred
to the Veterinary Emergency Center in Langhorne.

# Golden Grange Kennels
(609) 324-3647
134 Chesterfield Georgetown Rd
(@ Hwy 528)
Trenton, NJ 08650
www.goldengrange.com
**Hours:** Mon – Fri 8 AM – 11 PM
        Sat 8 AM – 5 PM,
        Sun 11 AM – 2 PM
        Mon – Fri 2 – 7 PM
**Payment:** Checks
**Price Range:** $$
This boarding, grooming, and training facility is the legacy of a
golden retriever named Brigadier, who inspired Joe and Karen
Mosner to move out to the country so they could have more
dogs, and ultimately open their own dog-care facility. With a
30-dog max, this state-of-the-art facility offers luxury boarding
($23 a night), positive-reinforcement training, and basic groom-
ing ($45). The kennels, which are cleaned several times a day,
are housed in a modern red barn. Joe teaches both group and
private classes, which range from beginner to advanced-
competition level, in the bright, spacious indoor training ring.

# Hamilton Veterinary Clinic

(609) 888-3400
18 E Park Ave
(@ S Broad St)
Trenton, NJ 08610
www.hamiltonveterinaryhospital.myvetonline.com
**Hours:** Mon – Thu 8 AM – 6 PM, Fri 8 AM – 5 PM
Sat 8 AM – 12 PM
**Payment:** Credit Cards, Checks
**Price Range:** $$

Dog and cat obstetrics, geriatric care, and canine cardiology
are some of the specialties practiced by this team of five
veterinarians and half a dozen vet techs. Dental exams and eye
care are also available. The waiting room stocks special-diet
pet foods and basic supplies like ear wash and nail trimmers.
Appointments for surgery should be made two to three weeks
in advance while a routine exam ($40) requires a week's
notice. After-hours emergencies are referred to the Veterinary
Specialty & Emergency Center near the Neshaminy Mall.

# Hazel & Hannah's Pawtisserie

(609) 921-7387
16 Witherspoon St
(@ Nassau St)
Princeton, NJ 08542
www.pawtisserie.com
**Hours:** Mon – Fri 10:30 AM – 6:30 PM
Sat 11 AM – 6 PM, Sun 12 PM – 5 PM
**Payment:** Credit Cards
**Price Range:** $$$

Fresh flowers, soft jazz, and the smell of home-cooked treats
lure pet and person alike into this homey shop. Wholesome
ingredients, including apple sauce, canola oil, carob, carrots,
garlic, honey, maple syrup, oats, peanut butter, and even sun-
dried tomatoes are among the ingredients in these delicious
confections. Special-occasion cakes and pastries make this
shop one of a kind. Best of all — there are no artificial colors,
flavors, or preservatives baked into any of the store's products. High-quality leashes, pet beds and outdoorsy supplies
like doggie backpacks are piled next to the bakery counter.
Hannah, the Rhodesian Ridgeback that started it all, would
approve.

## Hopewell Valley Kennel

(609) 466-4315
128 Lambertville Hopewell Rd
(@ Stony Brook Rd)
Hopewell, NJ 08525
**Hours:** Mon – Sat 9 AM – 12 PM
**Payment:** Checks
**Price Range:** $

You can't argue with the price ($20) or the five walks each pup gets a day at Hopewell. This climate-controlled 48-dog boarding facility offers indoor/outdoor kennels. You can bring toys, food, and bedding for your dog — quilts and blankets are preferred, although they will accept smallish beds. The two friendly staff members administer medication, food, and water. And the owner lives on the premises, providing 24-hour care and supervision. Playtime is available for a small charge. Holidays book up early, so plan as far in advance as possible.

## Hopewell Veterinary Group Inc.

(609) 466-0131
230 Hopewell Pennington Rd
(@ Van Dyke Rd)
Hopewell, NJ 08525
**Hours:** Mon – Fri 8 AM – 8 PM, Some Sat AM appts
Walk-in Hours Mon – Fri 1 – 2 PM, 7 – 8 PM
**Payment:** Checks
**Price Range:** $

Seven vets and a friendly support staff work together in this spacious facility to meet the needs of their four-legged, winged, and exotic patients. In addition to routine exams ($30), general procedures and surgeries, this facility also offers dental work under anesthesia. For after-hours emergencies, the automated phone system provides callers with numbers to reach on-call veterinarians. Prescription Diet dog foods can be purchased in the office. Appointments are usually booked about a week out. Bonus: If you take your pup in for vaccinations, the checkup is free.

## Joanna's Pet Portraits

(856) 795-1155
jlern@comcast.net
www.sjhorse.com/joanna
**Hours:** By Appt
**Payment:** Checks
**Price Range:** $$

Word of mouth coupled with a nod from *Philadelphia*
magazine for Best Animal Portraits keeps Joanna Lerner's
services in high demand. Lerner's been a pet Picasso for nearly
two decades, turning out commissioned pastel portraits of
purebreds and mutts alike. Residing in the affluent southern
New Jersey suburbs, Lerner has her share of well-to-do clients,
but thanks to her relatively reasonable prices ($500 for a 20 by
26-inch) even those on a bit more of a budget can immortalize
their pup in a painting. Joanna works solely from a photo of
your pet, so be sure to choose a flattering one.

## K-9 Kare Korner

(856) 783-1344
409 N White Horse Pike
(near Evesham Rd)
Magnolia, NJ  08049
www.k-9karekorner.com
**Hours:** Mon – Sat 9 AM – 5 PM
**Payment:** Credit Cards
**Price Range:** $$

With products stocked from top to bottom of each aisle, K-9
Kare Korner is a one-stop shop for all your pet product needs.
Serving Southern New Jersey for over 21 years, K-9 prides
itself on superior service and vast array of items, from oatmeal
shampoos and pet foods, to grooming supplies and bedding.
Customer satisfaction is their number-one priority. If you can't
find what you're looking for, ask a staff member and they will
track it down for you or special order it if they don't carry it.

## Lambertville Animal Clinic

(609) 397-3657
66 York St
(@ Rte 29)
Lambertville, NJ 08530
**Hours:** Mon, Wed 8 AM – 7 PM
        Tue, Thu – Fri 8 AM – 5 PM
        Sat 8:30 AM – 11:30 AM
**Payment:** Credit Cards, Checks
**Price Range:** $$
Standard procedures, exams (starting at $40 for newcomers) and routine surgeries are available, as is dental care under anesthesia. Prescription Diet–brand dog food is available for purchase in the lobby, as are function-over-fashion collars and medicated shampoos. Emergencies are referred to the Veterinary & Specialty Emergency Center in Langhorne, PA. Lambertville is one of the few area vets that can usually accommodate same-day appointments.

## Lawrence Animal Hospital

(609) 924-2293
3975 Princeton Pike
(@ Provinceline Rd)
Princeton, NJ 08540
www.vetcor.com/princeton/
**Hours:** Mon – Thu 7 AM – 7 PM
        Fri 7 AM – 6 PM
        Sat 8 AM – 1 PM
**Payment:** Credit Cards, Checks
**Price Range:** $$
Part of the 140-member Vetcor network, this 50-plus-year-old facility offers out-patient surgery, neutering/spaying, vaccinations, nutritional counseling, and dentistry. Emergencies are referred to Langhorne's Emergency Clinic. Science Diet, Hill's, and Prescription Diet are sold in the lobby. New clients receive 10 percent off their initial exam. Call three to four days in advance to schedule an appointment.

## Nottingham Animal Hospital

(609) 587-0222
395 Rte 33
(@ Hwy 533)
Trenton, NJ 08619
www.nottinghamvets.com
**Hours:** Mon – Thu 9 AM – 7 PM
　　　　Fri 9 AM – 6 PM, Sat 9 AM – 1 PM
**Payment:** Credit Cards, Checks
**Price Range:** $$$

This family-friendly, multivet practice is housed in a white
country cottage, where you'll find a glowing aquarium as
the centerpiece of the waiting room. Dental work, vaccina-
tions, preventative medicine, microchipping, and behavior
counseling are just a sampling of the clinic's offerings. They
keep space in their daily schedule to accommodate pups with
pressing health concerns, but routine exams typically require
a day's notice. Basic surgeries can often be scheduled within
a week. After-hours emergencies are referred to the Veterinary
Surgical and Diagnostic Specialists.

## Paws Pet Grooming & Supplies

(609) 586-9860
1905 Highway 33
(W of George Dye Rd)
Trenton, NJ 08690
**Hours:** Tue 9 AM – 8 PM
　　　　Wed – Sat 9 AM – 5 PM
**Payment:** Credit Cards, Checks
**Price Range:** $$

If you like the scent of pennyroyal, you'll adore Paws Pet.
Boasting an impressive line of grooming shampoos, this salon
takes the grooming process a step further, with sudsing
infusions such as aloe, oatmeal, and lavender. Even whitening
shampoos are available to brighten light coats. Owner and
groomer Amy Butler does hand scissoring, giving each client
her undivided attention as she performs breed-standard and
custom cuts. Dogs are dried with forced-air dryers, no cage
dryers are used. With grooming starting around $40, prices are
competitive with most area salons. Paws Pet offers extended
Tuesday hours to accommodate 9 – 5'ers. Call a couple of
days in advance to book an appointment.

## Pennington Veterinary Clinic at Pennytown

(609) 466-8402
53 Pennington Hopewell Rd
Pennington, NJ 08534
**Hours:** Mon – Wed 8 AM – 5 PM
　　　　Thu 9 AM – 5 PM
　　　　Sat 9 AM – 12 PM
**Payment:** Credit Cards, Checks
**Price Range:** $$

With a pharmacy at the facility and Prescription Diet–brand dog food for sale, this clinic strives to meet basic needs with minimum fuss. Three part-time vets perform spaying/neutering, dental work, check-ups ($50), vaccinations, and other standard procedures. As a special bonus for dogs getting a checkup, Pennington throws in a nail clip, and teeth cleaning (tartar scraping) for well-behaved pets that do not require anesthesia. For emergencies and special services, patients are referred to Langhorne. Same- or next-day appointments can usually be accommodated.

## Pet Valu

www.petvalu.com
**Hours:** Mon – Sat 9 AM – 9 PM
　　　　Sun 10 AM – 5 PM
**Payment:** Checks, Credit Cards
**Price Range:** $/$$

## Pet Valu: Cherry Hill

(856) 216-8455
1469 Brace Rd
Plot E Site 306
(between Kresson & Berlin Rds)
Cherry Hill, NJ 08034

## Pet Valu: Laurel Springs

(856) 309-1430
1216 Chews Landing Rd Suite E-21
(between Hilder Ln & Lincon Dr)
Laurel Springs, NJ 08012

## Pet Valu: Marlton

(856) 810-9595
744 W Rte 70
(off N Cropwell Rd)
Marlton, NJ 08053

## Pet Valu: Sewell

(856) 582-6612
380 Egg Harbor Rd
Ste C10
(between Greentree & Trent Rds)
Sewell, NJ 08080

## Pet Valu: Sicklerville

(856) 629-3940
542 Berlin Cross Keys Rd
(off Chews Landing Williamstown Rd)
Sicklerville, NJ 08081

The Costco of pet stores, Pet Valu provides bulk pet supplies warehouse style. Items include fleece jackets, paw protectors, over 100 styles of pet beds, travel carriers and kennels, plus premium and private-label foods, as well as all of the usual pet-care staples. Toys, of all shapes and sizes, from humongous tug toys to itty-bitty squeaky balls, stretch as far as the eye can see. And they also stock user-friendly grooming products like the all-natural waterless bath. If you don't see what you want, you can browse their in-store catalog for specialty items. The staff is consistently friendly and knowledgeable.

## Petco

www.petco.com
**Payment:** Credit Cards, Checks
**Price Range:** $/$$/$$$

## Petco: Cherry Hill

(856) 488-0643
2230 Marlton Pike W, Ste 3
(west of Penn-Central Reading Seashore Lines)
Cherry Hill, NJ 08002
**Hours:** Mon – Sat 9 AM – 9 PM, Sun 10 AM – 7 PM

## Petco: Cinnaminson
(856) 303-0944
2501 Rte 130 S
(@ Meeting House Rd)
Cinnaminson, NJ  08077
**Hours:** Mon – Sat 9 AM – 10 PM, Sun 10 AM – 8 PM

## Petco: Deptford
(856) 384-9609
1730 Clements Bridge Rd
(between Almonesson Rd & Rte 42)
Deptford, NJ  08096
**Hours:** Mon – Sat 9 AM – 9 PM, Sun 10 AM – 6 PM

## Petco: Pennsauken
(856) 662-9692
7024 Kaighns Ave
(@ Browning Rd)
Pennsauken, NJ  08109
**Hours:** Mon – Sat 9 AM – 9 PM
          Sun 10 AM – 8 PM

## Petco: Princeton
(609) 252-0294
301 North Harrison St
(in the Princeton Shopping Center)
Princeton, NJ  08540
**Hours:** Mon – Fri 9 AM – 8 PM
          Sat 9 AM – 7 PM,
          Sun 10 AM – 6 PM

## Petco: Willingboro

(609) 877-9711
4318 Rte 130 N
(between Pennypacker Dr & Delanco Rd)
Willingboro, NJ 08046
**Hours:** Mon – Sat 9 AM – 9 PM
　　　　Sun 10 AM – 6 PM

For one-stop shopping it's hard to beat the convenience and value of this superstore with locations all over the country. Petco makes it their mission to provide customers with the food, supplements, and products they want for their animals. Their bed selection runs the gamut, from orthopedic mattresses, along with sheets and throws, to chaises that would do an interior decorator proud. Get a P.A.L.S. (Petco Animal Lovers Save) card to take advantage of discounts; you may also want to check out their Top Dog program, which offers even greater saving to their most loyal customers. Check the listing for each store's hours and specific service offerings.

## PetSmart

www.petsmart.com
**Payment:** Credit Cards, Checks
**Price Range:** $/$$/$$$

## PetSmart: Cherry Hill

(856) 910-1400
2135 Rte 38, Ste B
(between Haddonfield Rd & Cherry Hill Mall Dr)
Cherry Hill, NJ 08002
**Hours:** Mon – Sat 9 AM – 9 PM, Sun 10 AM – 6 PM

## PetSmart: Deptford

(856) 853-0042
1800 Clements Bridge Rd, Ste. 1
(between Almonesson Rd & Rte 42)
Woodbury, NJ 08096
**Hours:** Mon – Sat 9 AM – 9 PM, Sun 10 AM – 6 PM

## PetSmart: Moorestown

(856) 439-9899
1331 N Nixon Dr
(off Lenola Rd, @Collins Rd)
Moorestown, NJ 08057
**Hours:** Mon – Sat 9 AM – 9 PM, Sun 10 AM – 6 PM

## PetSmart: Princeton

(609) 520-9200
111 Nassau Park Blvd
(off Rte 1)
Princeton, NJ 08540
**Hours:** Mon – Sat 8 AM – 9 PM, Sun 10 AM – 6 PM

This standout superstore is to pet owners what Home Depot is
to homeowners. PetSmart stocks an unbelievably wide range
of products that will meet almost any budget. They carry the
better dog food brands — including Bil-Jac. And whenever
possible, they offer all-natural options in their selection of
treats, supplements and skin products. A viewing window
allows see-for-yourself grooming so you don't have to worry
about what happens behind closed doors. They get major
points for promoting their adoptions all the time. And they
have a staff that's always available to advise you and to help
you find what you need. It's places like PetSmart that give
superstores a good name. Check the listing for each store's
hours and specific service offerings.

## Pierson Creek Kennels

(888)875-8379; (609) 397-5783
1484 Rte 179
(E of Music Mountain Blvd)
Lambertville, NJ 08530
www.piersoncreekkennels.com
**Hours:** Mon – Sat 8 AM – 6 PM, Sun 12 PM – 6 PM
        Closed for pickup/drop-off Mon – Fri 12 PM – 3 PM
**Payment:** Checks
**Price Range:** $$

Night lights, piped-in music, playtime, and central heat and air are just a few of the amenities pups enjoy at Pierson Creek Kennels. This boarding facility is neat and tidy, with red brick walks, green lawns, and crisp white buildings. For $20 per day, dogs stay in one of thirty-five 6 x 5-foot runs, and are walked four times a day. Pierson Creek takes pride in the extra care and attention they give to older dogs. They will accommodate special diet requests and administer medications. Basic grooming is also available. The owners, who live on-site, offer 24-hour service and care. Additionally, a veterinarian is on-call 24/7.

## Plainsboro Township Dog Park
(609) 799-0099, x10
Scotts Corner Rd
(@ Dey Rd)
Plainsboro, NJ 08536
**Hours:** Every Day: Sunrise to Sunset
**Payment:** Free

This one-acre, fenced-in dog park is all the rage among Plainsboro dog aficionados. Parking, port-a-potties, and benches are available on-site, as are gloves and bags. Be sure to bring your own water; chasing your own tail can be thirsty work. Take note: Your dog must remain on leash until you are inside the play area. All dogs must have a valid license and be current on their vaccinations — failure to comply with regulations may result in a fine.

## Precious Pets
**Payment:** Credit Cards, Checks
**Price Range:** $$

## Precious Pets: Burlington
(609) 239-6800
1091 Rte 130 S
(between Illinois & States Aves)
Burlington, NJ 08016
**Hours:** Mon – Sat 9 AM – 9 PM
           Sun 10 AM – 6 PM

## Precious Pets: Hightstown
(609) 448-8444
625 Mercer St
(@ Airport Rd)
Hightstown, NJ 08520
**Hours:** Mon – Sat 9 AM – 10 PM
Sun 10 AM – 6 PM

## Precious Pets: Trenton
(609) 771-1448
1510 Pennington Rd
(@ N Olden Ave)
Trenton, NJ 08618
**Hours:** Mon – Sat 9 AM – 9 PM
Sun 10 AM – 6 PM

Self-styled animal nuts, Precious Pets offers 10 percent off your purchases at any one of their three locations if you use their online coupon. In business for more 10 years, the store stocks a wealth of supplies for all types of animals. Dog offerings include foods like Innova and Wellness ($19 for a 20-pound bag) and products such as St. John's Natural Toothpaste — appropriately peanut-butter flavored. If you don't see the brand you want, be sure to ask — they stock extra in the garage. You can also place orders online.

## Princeton Animal Hospital
(609) 520-2000
726 Alexander Rd
(@ Roszel Rd)
Princeton, NJ 08540
www.myvetonline.com/website/princetonanimalhospital
**Hours:** Mon – Fri 6 AM – 8:30 PM, Sat 7 AM – 4 PM,
Sun 8 AM – 4 PM, Doctors On-call 24/7.
**Payment:** Credit Cards, Checks
**Price Range:** $$
Housed in a red-brick colonial facade with white columns, this animal hospital has been catering to dogs, cats, and pocket pets since 1988. Doctors Jim and Terry Miele, the husband-and-wife team that owns and runs this practice, also run Carnegie Cat Clinic and Plainsboro – West Windsor Veterinary Associates. With a roster of ten veterinarians, PAC offers basic exams ($48), vaccinations, routine surgeries, radiology, lab work, prescriptions, dental, and eye care as part of their mission to provide well-rounded family-pet health care.

Always accommodating, they offer late weekday and weekend hours for nine-to-five types. Schedule exams at least a week in advance — emergencies need no appointment.

# Puppergarten
(609) 730-0304
26 Woosamonsa Rd
(@ Hwy 31)
Pennington, NJ 08534
www.puppergarten.com
**Hours:** By Appt
**Payment:** Checks
**Price Range:** $$

Professional trainer, groomer, and vet tech Megan Miller has more than 25 years of experience with dogs. Using positive-reinforcement techniques, she offers classes for dogs of all ages. Her courses, starting with puppy kindergarten ($115), are completed in six one-hour sessions. She also offers private lessons at clients' homes ($95 an hour) to address issues like chewing, housebreaking, aggression, and jumping. She does not believe in the use of choke or pronged collars. You can read about some of her success stories on her Web site.

# Quaker Bridge Animal Hospital
(609) 586-7799
3710 Quakerbridge Rd
(between Youngs Rd & Nami Ln)
Trenton, NJ 08619
**Hours:** Mon – Tue 8:30 AM – 3:45 PM
Wed 8:30 AM – 3:30 PM
Thu – Fri 8:30 AM – 12:30 PM
Sat 8:30 AM – 12:15 PM
Mon & Fri 7 – 9 PM
**Payment:** Checks
**Price Range:** $

If you're on a budget, Quaker Bridge Animal Hospital is worth a look. The full range of basic surgeries, vaccinations, dental care, routine exams ($24), and general procedures are offered at prices slightly below the area norm. The warm manner of Dr. Smith, the sole veterinarian and owner of Quaker Bridge, gives a nice, personal touch to the otherwise clinical setting.

After-hours emergencies are referred to Columbus Central Veterinary Hospital. Appointments can usually be scheduled within a week.

# Reigning Dogs and Cats Grooming and Massage
(609) 588-9300
950 Hwy 33
(between Deerwood Ave & Paxson Ave)
Trenton, NJ 08690
**Hours:** Mon – Fri 10:30 AM – 7 PM
**Payment:** Credit Cards
**Price Range:** $$$

Part dog spa, part gourmet pet deli and bakery, this trendy boutique pays homage to the royal canine in your life with massage treatments ($35 for 35 minutes), hydrotherapy, teeth cleaning, grooming ($65 for a bath and cut), and decorative nail-art procedures. Dogs are dried in cages with a no-heat, octopus dryer. More than 80 types of treats are baked weekly to tempt your pup's palate: Puppy Pizzas with lamb or chicken ($10), beef or turkey meatballs and Woofie Burgers are all made with human-grade ingredients.

# Rosedale Mills
(609) 737-2008
101 State Hwy 31
(@ Titus Mill Rd)
Pennington, NJ 08534
www.rosedalemills.com
**Hours:** Mon – Thu 8 AM – 6 PM, Fri 8 AM – 7 PM
Sat 8 AM – 5 PM
Sun 9 AM – 4 PM
**Payment:** Credit Cards, Checks
**Price Range:** $$

Proclaiming themselves "America's country store," Rosedale Mills, in business since 1950, offers something for everyone — from dog lovers and equestrians, to gardeners and bird lovers. Beautifully painted doghouses, crates, carriers, collars, leashes, bowls, vitamins, grooming supplies, and beds are just a sampling of the bonanza of dog goods available. They have one of the biggest display of Greenies ever seen. Dog foods range from nutritious-commercial brands to high-end, healthy choices. You may also want to check out their full-service grooming salon, The Pet Parlor. Other offerings include swing sets, lawn mowers, livestock food, and gazebos.

# Trenton Veterinary Hospital

(609) 394-8171
697 Pennington Ave
(@ Mellon St)
Trenton, NJ 08618
**Hours:** Mon – Fri 11 AM – 1 PM
        Sat 9 AM – 12 PM
        Mon, Tue, Thu 4 PM – 5:30 PM
**Payment:** Credit Cards, Checks
**Price Range:** $

Thirty years of experience back up the solid reputation of Dr. Batts, who strives to keep costs of standard procedures, checkups (starting at $31), and surgeries at an affordable level. He also offers teeth cleaning, but only under anesthesia. Prescription Diet–brand pet food is available for purchase, and prescriptions can be filled on-site. Appointments can usually be scheduled within a day or two of calling. Most emergencies, especially after-hours, are referred to the Veterinary & Specialty Emergency Center in Langhorne, PA.

# Veterinary Care Center

(609) 890-6266
3100 Quakerbridge Rd
(between Macon Dr & Brookwood Rd)
Trenton, NJ 08619
**Hours:** Mon 8 AM – 7 PM, Tue 8 AM – 4 PM
        Wed – Thu 8 AM – 7 PM
        Fri 8 AM – 5 PM, Sat 8 AM – 1 PM
**Payment:** Credit Cards, Checks
**Price Range:** $

Conveniently located in a Trenton strip mall, this small clinic minimizes hassles with easy scheduling, affordable exams and on-site products. David Horn, DVM, has owned and operated this practice for eight years, working alongside his associate Dr. Gallager. In addition to the requisite treatment rooms and surgery room, VCC features a large outside run for those pups staying longer than an hour or two. Available products include food. Exams start at $40. For a weekday appointment, a couple of days' notice is necessary; schedule a week out for evenings or weekends.

## Weber's Boarding and Training
(609) 452-8081
3440 Us Highway 1
(between Nassau Park Blvd & Emmons Dr)
Princeton, NJ 08540
**Hours:** Mon – Fri 8 AM – 6 PM
　　　　Sat 8 AM – 5 PM
　　　　Sun 9 AM – 11 PM
**Payment:** Checks
**Price Range:** $

Boot camp for boarded pups, Weber's combines vacation care with obedience training. The two-week basic-training course involves discipline and choke collars — no treats. Your pup will get several 15-minute outdoor breaks a day (weather permitting). Be sure to bring your pet's blanket or small bed, they don't keep any on hand. However, food is included. Staff will give meds to your pup for an extra charge. And should your pup feel under the weather, Weber's has a vet standing, by at all times. Rates are reasonable — and people know it, so book early.

## West Trenton Animal Hospital
(609) 771-0995
568 Grand Ave
(between W Upper Ferry Rd & Summit Ave)
West Trenton, NJ 08628
www.westtrentonanimalhosp.com
**Hours:** Mon – Fri 7 AM – 7 PM
　　　　Sat 8 AM – 12 PM
**Payment:** Credit Cards, Checks
**Price Range:** $$$

There is definitely a family-type vibe among the staff, who will do everything they possibly can to accommodate you and your animal, even make house calls (a surcharge does apply). West Trenton is so popular that it takes an average of three weeks to get an appointment but given their loyal following, people clearly think it's worth the wait. The vets perform routine exams ($44), treatments and surgeries, as well as preventative treatment and dental care (under anesthesia). High-tech radiology and geriatric services are the specialties of this hospital. And when the worst happens, it's comforting to know that they offer numerous end-of-life services, including burial and cremation.

## Whiskers & Tails

(609) 586-4046
27 George Dye Rd
(@ Nottingham Way)
Trenton, NJ 08690
**Hours:** Mon – Fri 8 AM – 4:30 PM, Sat 9 AM – 4 PM
**Payment:** Credit Cards, Checks
**Price Range:** $$

Though not small — there are four full-time groomers on staff — this shop takes a boutique approach to grooming, using a variety of hypoallergenic, fragrance-free and other specialty grooming products. Shampoos and such can be purchased on-site, should you become inspired to go the home-bathing route. For a medium-sized pup, a bath, brush, trim, ear cleaning, and nail clip costs $50. Groomers carefully supervise dogs being cage dried. The staff can only accommodate special requests, such as lamb cuts for poodles, when time permits. Short-haired cats are welcome, but the facility no longer accepts longhaired felines.

# Wilmington & Surrounding

## ALTERNATIVE PRODUCTS/SERVICES

**Wilmington**
Happy Dog Healthy Dog
Windcrest Animal Hospital & Boarding Kennel

## ANIMAL HOSPITALS & VET CLINICS

**Wilmington**
Windcrest Animal Hospital & Boarding Kennel

## CAT SERVICES/PRODUCTS AVAILABLE

**All Neighborhoods**
Tails and Whiskers Pet Sitting

**Christianna**
Petco: Christianna
PetSmart: Christianna

**Newark**
Concord Pet Foods & Supplies: Capitol Trail
Concord Pet Foods & Supplies: Suburban Dr
Petco: Newark

**Wilmington**
Concord Pet Foods & Supplies: Concord Pike
Concord Pet Foods & Supplies: Faulkland Rd
Concord Pet Foods & Supplies: Marsh Rd
PetSmart: Wilmington

# CITY DOG PICKS

**Lewes**
Home Away From Home Boarding & Kennel

**New Castle**
Pike Creek Carousel Park

**Newark**
Academy of Dog Training & Agility
Playtime Doggie Daycare & Pet Salon

**Wilmington**
Happy Dog Healthy Dog

# DOG BOARDING

**Lewes**
Home Away From Home Boarding & Kennel
Never Never Land Kennel

**Newark**
Playtime Doggie Daycare & Pet Salon

**Wilmington**
Pooch Palace Doggie Daycare
Windcrest Animal Hospital & Boarding Kennel

# DOG DAY CARE

**Newark**
Playtime Doggie Daycare & Pet Salon

**Wilmington**
Pooch Palace Doggie Daycare

# DOG GROOMING

**Christiana**
Petco: Christiana
PetSmart: Christiana

**Lewes**
Home Away From Home Boarding & Kennel
Never Never Land Kennel

**Newark**
Petco: Newark
Playtime Doggie Daycare & Pet Salon

**Wilmington**
PetSmart: Wilmington
Pooch Palace Doggie Daycare
Windcrest Animal Hospital & Boarding Kennel

## DOG PARKS & TRAILS

**New Castle**
Pike Creek Carousel Park

## DOG TRAINING

**Newark**
Academy of Dog Training & Agility
PetSmart: Christiana
Playtime Doggie Daycare & Pet Salon

## DOG WALKING/PET SITTING

**Middletown**
Tails and Whiskers Pet Sitting

## LOW-COST VACCINATION CLINICS

**Christiana**
Petco: Christiana

**Newark**
Petco: Newark

**Wilmington**
PetSmart: Wilmington

## ON-SITE PET ADOPTIONS

**Christiana**
Petco: Christiana

**Newark**
Petco: Newark
PetSmart: Christiana

**Wilmington**
PetSmart: Wilmington
Windcrest Animal Hospital & Boarding Kennel

## PET-SUPPLY STORES

**Christiana**
Petco: Christiana
PetSmart: Christiana

**Newark**
Concord Pet Foods & Supplies: Capitol Trail
Concord Pet Foods & Supplies: Peoples Plaza
Concord Pet Foods and Supplies: Suburban Dr
Petco: Newark

**Wilmington**
Concord Pet Foods & Supplies: Concord Pike
Concord Pet Foods & Supplies: Faulkland Rd
Concord Pet Foods & Supplies: Marsh Rd
Happy Dog Healthy Dog
Pet Valu: Wilmington
PetSmart: Wilmington

## PHOTOGRAPHY/PAINTINGS

**Christiana**
Petco: Christiana

## SELF-SERVE DOG GROOMING

**Stanton**
Dogomat

# General Listings

## Academy of Dog Training & Agility
(302) 588-4636
107F Albe Dr
(near Old Baltimore Pike)
Newark, DE 19702
www.academyofdogtraining.com
**Hours:** Check Web site for class times
**Payment:** Credit Cards
**Price Range:** $$

Owner Don Brown has a hand in every class offered at his popular academy. He trains through positive reinforcement, using a clicker. Classes range from beginning obedience to advanced show-ring handling, as well as rally and agility training. Classes are held both indoors, in the academy's air-conditioned facility, complete with a matted floor, and outside when weather permits. The academy also holds regular social mixers for pets and their people to help cultivate pet-person bonds. If your pup is the nonsocial type, Don also offers private lessons. Most classes run for eight weeks and cost between $80 and $100. Class schedules and applications are available on the Web site.

## Concord Pet Foods & Supplies
www.concordpet.com
**Hours:** Mon – Sat 9 AM – 9 PM
          Sun 10 AM – 5 PM
**Payment:** Credit Cards, Checks
**Price Range:** $/$$/$$$

## Concord Pet Foods & Supplies: Capitol Trail
(302) 737-8982
1450 Capitol Trl #15
(off Kirkwood Hwy)
Newark, DE
www.concordpet.com

## Concord Pet Foods & Supplies: Concord Pike
(302) 478-8966
3703 Concord Pike

(@ Prospect Ave)
Wilmington, DE  19803

## Concord Pet Foods & Supplies: Faulkland Rd

(302) 995-2255
1720 Faulkland Rd
(off Centre Rd)
Wilmington, DE  19805

## Concord Pet Foods & Supplies: Marsh Rd

(302) 477-1995
1722 Marsh Rd
(off Wilson Rd)
Wilmington, DE  19810

## Concord Pet Foods & Supplies: Peoples Plaza

(302) 836-5787
238 Peoples Plaza
(off Glasgow Ave)
Newark, DE  19702

## Concord Pet Foods and Supplies: Suburban Dr

(302) 368-2959
312 Suburban Dr
(in the Suburban Plaza Shopping Center)
Newark, DE  19711
Concord takes one-stop shopping to a whole new level —
stocking everything from foods (Wellness, Innova, and Natura)
to Wee Wee pads ($40 for 100) to Outward Hound life jackets.
They also have a full line of Booda toys, joint supplements,
car seats, brushes and shampoos, as well as Nylabone chews
($2 to $5 each). And if you feel like turning your backyard
into a nature sanctuary, they also offer supplies for squirrels,
deer, birds, and rodents, as well as items for reptiles, pigs, and,
of course, dogs. You can shop online or head to one of their
stores to take advantage of their excellent customer service.

## Dogomat

(302) 999-8843
109 Main St
(@ Chestnut St)
Stanton, DE  19804
**Hours:** Mon 9 AM – 3 PM, Tue 2 AM – 8 PM
        Wed – Sun 9 AM – 3 PM
**Payment:** Credit Cards, Checks

**Price Range:** $$

Housed in a cheerful brick building, Dogomat is great for those who want to scrub their dog — but don't want the fur-clogged drain and aching back that bathing your pup in your tub can cause. And your dog will appreciate their treat-filled "doggie salad bar." Each of the self-serve stations comes equipped with a four-foot wide waist-high tub, a flexible hose with pre-set lukewarm water and a professional cool-air blow dryer. Dogomat also has eight specialty shampoos (including hypoallergenic, oatmeal, and flea control), towels and plenty of combs and brushes. At $12 a visit, the shop stays pretty busy — and they don't take appointments — so your best bet is to get there when they open.

# Happy Dog Healthy Dog

(302) 428-1919
1825 Delaware Ave
(@ Laurel St)
Wilmington, DE 19806
www.happydoghealthydog.com
**Hours:** Tue – Fri 10 AM – 7 PM, Sat – Sun 10 AM – 3 PM
**Payment:** Credit Cards, Checks
**Price Range:** $$

This one-stop pup-wellness destination offers delicious whole-some treats, baked by owner Diane Mayer, who also has a hand in educating dog owners in the art of canine massage and dog nutrition with her on-site classes. (After attending Dog Food 101, you may never feed commercial again.) The store is stocked with environmentally friendly goodies like Poop Happens Bags alongside Bodhi Toys and Wagwear products. Diane also holds greyhound adoptions twice a month. An environmentally friendly, state-of-the-art canine hydrotherapy facility, designed with the help of a feng shui master, is in the works.

# Home Away From Home Boarding & Grooming Kennel

(302) 684-8576
18600 Raven's Way
(@ Narrow Rd)
Lewes, DE 19958
www.atbeach.com/services/homeaway/

**Hours:** Mon – Fri 8:30 AM – 5:30 PM
Sat 8:30 AM – 4 PM, Sun 4 AM – 6 PM
**Payment:** Credit Cards, Checks
**Price Range:** $$

Owner/operator Denise Irwin knows how to cater to the vacationing pup at this luxury dog resort. Indoor/outdoor runs, comfortable bedding, soothing music and a grooming salon are a few of the amenities your pet will enjoy, along with a kiddie pool for summertime splashing and swimming. Rates vary based on breed and size of pet. Administering meds is extra. And if you want your pup to get some social time, for a nominal fee you can schedule in playtime with the resident golden retriever. After-hours drop-off and pickup are available for a $50 fee.

## Neverland Kennel & Cattery

(302) 645-6140
34377 Neverland Ln
(off Rte 1)
Lewes, DE  19958
www.neverlandkennel.com
**Hours:** Mon – Sun 8:30 AM – 12 PM, 4 PM – 5:30 PM
**Payment:** Credit Cards
**Price Range:** $$

Neverland Kennel has been catering to the hydrant-loving set since 1975. With climate-controlled kennels and private outdoor runs, it is clear that pet comfort is the number one priority here. Other offerings include positive-reinforcement training and full-service grooming — with a fluff dry. Rates run from $21 to $25 per day, depending on the season. There's a two-day minimum for weekends from May through September, and a four-day minimum stay during major holidays. Applications are available online.

## Pet Valu: Wilmington

(302) 992-9900
1710 W Newport Pike
(off Glenmore Dr)
Wilmington, DE  19804
www.petvalu.com

**Hours:** Mon – Sat 9 AM – 9 PM
Sun 10 AM – 5 PM
**Payment:** Credit Cards, Checks
**Price Range:** $$

The Costco of pet stores, Pet Valu provides bulk pet supplies warehouse style. Items include fleece jackets, paw protectors, over 100 styles of pet beds, travel carriers and kennels, plus premium and private-label foods, as well as all of the usual pet-care staples. Toys, of all shapes and sizes, from humongous tug toys to itty-bitty squeaky balls, stretch as far as the eye can see. And they also stock user-friendly grooming products like the all-natural waterless bath. If you don't see what you want, you can browse their in-store catalog for specialty items. The staff is consistently friendly and knowledgeable.

## Petco
www.petco.com
**Payment:** Credit Cards, Checks
**Price Range:** $/$$/$$$

## Petco: Christiana
(302) 894-0290
200 Center Blvd
(between Stanton Christiana Rd & Christiana Mall Blvd)
Christiana, DE 19702
**Hours:** Mon – Sat 8 AM – 9:30 PM
Sun 10 AM – 8 PM

## Petco: Newark
(302) 894-0290
200 Center Blvd
(off Stanton Christiana Rd)
Newark, DE 19702
**Hours:** Mon – Sat 9 AM – 10 PM
Sun 10 AM – 7 PM

For one-stop shopping it's hard to beat the convenience and value of this superstore with locations all over the country. Petco makes it their mission to provide customers with the food, supplements and products they want for their animals. Their bed selection runs the gamut, from orthopedic mattresses, along with sheets and throws, to chaises that would do an interior decorator proud. Get a P.A.L.S. (Petco Animal Lovers Save) card to take advantage of discounts; you may also want to check out their Top Dog program, which offers even greater saving to their most loyal customers. Check the listing for each store's hours and specific service offerings.

## PetSmart

www.petsmart.com
**Payment:** Credit Cards, Checks
**Price Range:** $/$$/$$$

## PetSmart: Christiana

(302) 266-6170
1291 Churchmans Rd
(between Ogleton Stanton Rd & Continental Dr)
Newark, DE 19713
**Hours:** Mon – Sat 9 AM – 9 PM
Sun 10 AM – 6 PM

## PetSmart: Wilmington

(302) 475-0618
3010 Brandywine Pkwy
(off Naamans Rd)
Wilmington, DE 19803
**Hours:** Mon – Sat 8 AM – 9 PM
Sun 9 AM – 6 PM
**Payment:** Credit Cards, Checks
**Price Range:** $

This standout superstore is to pet owners what Home Depot is to homeowners. PetSmart stocks an unbelievably wide range of products that will meet almost any budget. They carry the better dog food brands — including Bil-Jac. And whenever possible, they offer all-natural options in their selection of treats, supplements and skin products. A viewing window allows see-for-yourself grooming so you don't have to worry about what happens behind closed doors. They get major points for promoting their adoptions all the time. And they have a staff that's always available to advise you and to help you find what you need. It's places like PetSmart that give superstores a good name. Check the listing for each store's hours and specific service offerings.

## Pike Creek Carousel Park

Limestone Rd
(@ Rte 7)
New Castle, DE
**Hours:** Every Day: Sunrise to Sunset
**Payment:** Free

Affectionately known as Bark Park, this huge facility inside
Carousel Park features an expansive grassy knoll with shade
trees and tables. Dogs may roam off leash, just as long as the
owner is keeping a close eye on them. There are plenty of trash
cans and water faucets, but bring baggies — and towels if your
pup's a swimmer. In the summer months dogs regularly dip into
Enchanted Lake. This is a favorite spot among dog lovers. Your
pet is sure to make some friends, and you just might too.

## Playtime Doggie Daycare & Pet Salon

(302) 368-3100
62 Albe Dr Suite A
(@ Old Baltimore Pike)
Newark, DE 19702
www.playtimedoggiedaycare.com
**Hours:** Mon 7 AM – 7 PM, Tue 7 AM – 5 PM,
            Wed – Fri 7 AM – 7 PM, Sat 9 AM – 5 PM
**Payment:** Credit Cards, Checks
**Price Range:** $$

It's always playtime at this daycare, grooming, and training
emporium. The cage-free atmosphere allows for plenty of group
playtime in the large, gymnasium-style playrooms. The separate
nap area features pillows, blankets, and soft classical music.
The grooming is also cage free and includes hydro-massage
bathing, a brush-out, ear cleaning, and nail trimming, topped
off with a fluff dry — all courtesy of the on-site master groom-
ers. Positive-reinforcement training classes include basic obedi-
ence and puppy courses. They also offer canine massage and
Scooby Doo– or Clifford-themed doggie parties, complete with
apple cinnamon cake and games like bobbing for hot dogs.

# Pooch Palace Doggie Daycare

(302) 456-7890
700-EL Cornell Dr
(@ Rogers Rd)
Wilmington, DE  19801
**Hours:** Mon – Fri 7 AM – 7 PM, Sat 8 AM – 5 PM
**Payment:** Credit Cards
**Price Range:**  $$

Pooch Palace Doggie Day Care is a king-sized 1500-square-foot spread, where the attentive staff makes sure that every dog gets the royal treatment. Separated into play groups by size and temperament, dogs enjoy free play in large runs, and are walked every two hours. Half-day sessions are $15; $20 for the full day. Boarding and grooming are also available. In addition to breed-specific styling by a master groomer, standard service includes shampooing, nail trimming and ear trimming/cleaning, a brush out, fluff dry, and a stylish bow or bandanna finish. Casual clips are also available. Grooming is by appointment only.

# Tails and Whiskers Pet Sitting

(302) 354-2607
40 West Mingle Wood Dr
(off Rte 71)
Middletown, DE  19709
www.tailsnwhiskers.net
**Hours:** By Appt
**Payment:** Credit Cards
**Price Range:**  $$

Whether you need your dog walked and fed, your mail collected while you're out of town, or just need someone to make a last-minute run for dog food, Tails and Whiskers can help. One of several friendly staff members can stop by once, twice, or three times a day to play with, walk, and feed your pet. Walks typically last 20 minutes, unless longer or shorter times are requested. They pride themselves on being flexible and accommodating; if there's a service you're interested in, Tails and Whiskers will work with you to implement it.

# Windcrest Animal Hospital & Boarding Kennel

(302) 998-2995
3705 Lancaster Pike
(@ Greenridge Rd)
Wilmington, DE 19805
www.windcrestanimal.com
**Hours:** Every Day: 24 Hours
**Payment:** Credit Cards
**Price Range:** $$
This state-of-the-art, 24-hour medical facility is also an all-inclusive boarding resort. Medical services include dermatology, dentistry, surgery, and cancer treatment as well as a host of other services. You can reserve time for a dog spa day that includes a massage and a bath with a blow dry. Boarded dogs lounge in their own runs, which are complete with heated floors. Sign your dog up for their VIP program, and she'll receive daily walks and playtime. Windcrest is home to "Save the Animals Adoption Center." Senior citizens (people, not dogs) get a 10 percent discount on services from 9 AM to 5 PM, Tuesday through Thursday.

# Cyber Dog

## B. A. Barker

www.babarker.com

**Payment:** Credit Cards

**Price Range:** $/$$

If knick knacks are your cup of tea, then go no farther. This site has it all. You can search by category or by breed, making this the perfect pit stop for the dog-obsessed shopper. Although B. A. Barker is geared more toward the dog lover than the dog, it does carry a limited selection of dog items — toys, tags, and the ever-popular edible rawhide greeting cards.

## Bark, The

www.thebark.com

**Payment:** Credit Cards

**Price Range:** $$

Hailed as the thinking person's dog magazine, this Berkeley-based quarterly magazine is an eloquently outspoken dog-rights advocate. From dog parks — with plenty of on-site tips on how to create and hold onto dog parks — to the horrors of puppy mills, *The Bark* always tells it like it is. And their book reviews are the best. You won't catch them using silly word coinages that are a little too *pawfect*. Check it out at the newsstand or on the Internet.

## Big Bark Bakery
(888) 3BOW WOW
www.bigbarkbakery.com
**Payment:** Credit Cards
**Price Range:** $$

Whether you want a three-tiered custom cake for your precious princess or Howlin' Good Biscuits ($6.50 for a one-pound bag) for your mellow mutt, Big Bark Bakery is the place to go for all of your pup-pastry needs. Everything is human-grade, and sugar-, salt-, and preservative-free. Other favorites include Dippity-Doo-Dads (peanut biscuits dipped in carob) and Tasty Twisters (peanut and honey cinnamon rolls). Cakes (starting at $18) are available in banana nut, apple cinnamon, and honey almond flavors, with a choice of cream cheese, honey, or cinnamon icing. These treats can be purchased through Big Bark's Web site and also through Whole Foods grocery stores in and around Dallas.

## Bow Wow Shop
(866) 855-4621
www.bowwowshop.com
**Payment:** Credit Cards
**Price Range:** $/$$

This purple-and-yellow Web site has some great deals on everything from "Canine Co-dependent" T-shirts to professional grooming tables and supplies. Paw- and leopard-print faux fur blankets are $29. Outdoor types will appreciate the Ruff Wear Life Vests, hunting coats ($30), first-aid kits ($46), and collar safety lights ($5). The treats seem more strange than sumptuous: low-fat Dixie's banana apple tarts and Dixie's salmon surprise are among the choices.

## Brown Kennel Supply Inc.
(800) 772-9028
www.brownkennelsupply.com
**Hours:** See Web site for dog show schedule
**Payment:** Credit Cards
**Price Range:** $$

With satisfaction as the primary goal, Brown Kennel Supply has truly gone to the dogs . . . but in a good way. Retired couple Don and Anna take their motor home on the dog show circuit every weekend — recently, they added agility shows to their schedule. Son Sean cooks the liver treats that are quickly gaining a cult following. Other favorites include the ever-popular "Bitches Britches" ($9), teeth scrapers ($4), baggies, rakes, and poop scoopers. They're always offering something new, such as top-of-the-line nose blackener or portable pet homes ($28 – $165). Go online to buy products or to find out when the Browns will arrive in your neighborhood.

## Canine Automotive Restraint Equipment (C.A.R.E)
(800) 352-0010

www.canineauto.com

**Payment:** Credit Cards

**Price Range:** $/$$/$$$

No more need for soccer-mom arm blocks when you take your dog on the road. Canine Automotive Restraint Equipment (C.A.R.E.) offers seat-belt harnesses (starting at $28) as well as barriers to keep dogs safe and secure in the car. Some of the higher-end canine safety systems include a discounted puppy-size restraint. They also offer truck restraints, seat covers (starting at $30), ramps, and window guards that allow dogs to enjoy fresh air without being able to stick their heads out of the vehicle.

## Canine Styles
www.caninestyles.com

**Payment:** Credit Cards

**Price Range:** $$$

The go-to groomer for New York's society dog set, Canine Styles has taken over the uber-hip Fetch! Pets as well as the petite-pup posh Karen For People and Pets. The resulting selection is beyond impressive. You will still find Styles classic equestrian-chic dog blankets ($60 – $100). The beach tote Straw Carrier ($95) is an absolute summer must-have. Top-of-the-line bath supplies will keep dogs sudsy clean and when you're done with the bath, you can wrap your pup up in the Hooded Bath Towel ($35 – $44). The bed selection includes Shabby Beds ($125 – $195), which are anything but, as well as retro-chic plaid cushions ($75 – $95).

## Chic Doggie by Corey

www.chicdog.com
**Payment:** Credit Cards
**Price Range:** $$$

This haute dog couture line is created by former investment banker Corey Gelman with the help of her model/muse Bear. The canine cashmere offerings include dog coats, scarves ($95), and blankets ($395), while the silver necklaces ($125 – $145) look great on you or your pooch. The Hermés-inspired dog carriers ($360) make perfect travel accessories; you can finish the look by accessorizing your pet with little doggie and kitty barrettes ($18 – $25). Celebs such as Madonna, Oprah, and Aerosmith's Steven Tyler are among Chic Doggie's clientele.

## Colorado Canines and Felines Too!

www.coloradocanines.com
**Payment:** Credit Cards
**Price Range:** $/$$/$$$

Luckily for the rest of us, this all-natural bakery and boutique is not just for Colorado canines. The Bear Bells ($7) probably won't get much use by anyone outside the Rockies, but the rest of the outdoor equipment — Ruff Wear Approach Packs to go on your dog, beacons ($13), first-aid kits ($46) — are great for outdoor types anywhere. Arfy's Peanut Butter Pussy Cats ($6) are among the tasty treats. The healthy dog food selection includes dry food (Chicken Meal and Brown Rice is $34 for a 30-pound bag) and canned food ($2 for a 13.2-ounce can of Merrick) as well as raw food and raw-food mixers (available for local delivery only). The search engine is not very powerful; you may have better luck browsing the menus to find what you want.

## Doctors Foster & Smith

(800) 381-7179
www.drsfostersmith.com
**Payment:** Credit Cards
**Price Range:** $/$$/$$$

For one-stop Internet shopping, it is hard to beat this vet-owned shop. The hospital-grade orthopedic beds (the Super Deluxe ranges from $90 to $190) are great for aging dogs, or those with aches and pains, while the Luxury Bolster Beds ($90 – $150) blend in with almost any decor. They also have a great selection of snacks and bones. If your dog suffers from food allergies, you might try their Pampered Pet Treats ($13). Clothing ranges from chic sweaters to casual golf shirts to Pet Wrap Vests (starting at $40) to costumes. You can also get your dog's meds here by having your vet call in or fax the prescription. (See Web site for instructions.)

## Dog Friendly

www.dogfriendly.com

If you're feeling guilty for leaving your dog home alone while you're stuck in the office, this Web site tells you not only what stores, restaurants, and hotels will welcome your dog, but also which employers allow dogs in the workplace. This city-specific resource is great for locals and travelers. Every place listed welcomes all sizes and all breeds — as long as they are well behaved.

## Dog Specialties

(214) 219-5555

www.dogspecialties.com

**Payment:** Credit Cards

**Price Range:**  $$$

Susie, Baxter, Sade, and Miss Daisy were the inspiration behind this eclectic boutique where the practical meets the whimsical. Products include animal-print coats, donut beds, posh polka-dotted carriers, ornate dog bowls, and all manner of bling-inspired leashes and collars. All products are dog-tested and dog-approved before being put on their shelves. Dog Specialties also offers a wide variety of dog-centric art work, doormats ($20 – $25), and bakery treats ($1 – $5) that smell so good you'll want to eat them yourself. Shop online if you can't make it to the store.

## Dog Outer Gear

(617) 569-8255

www.dogoutergear.com

**Payment:** Credit Cards, Checks

**Price Range:** $$

No matter the weather, D.O.G. (Dog Outer Gear) will keep your pup warm and dry. Manufactured in East Boston, all apparel is machine washable and dryable. Currently, there are five coat styles (starting at $30), in a variety of colors and sizes. Quality nonskid dog boots are also available to complete the inclement-weather ensemble. T-shirts (starting at $15) range from hip to cutesy, and you can order collars that spell "DOG" ($15) or your dog's name ($28) in Swarovski crystal. The Web site has helpful suggestions about the styles that best fit specific body types.

## Dog Pals

www.dogpals.com

An affordable alternative to day care, this community-service site aims to pair up dogs so that they can play while their people are away. With plenty of bulletin boards and chat areas, it's a great idea, and it seems to be slowly catching on.

## Dog Toys

(877) DOG-TOYS

www.dogtoys.com

**Payment:** Credit Cards

**Price Range:** $/$$/$$$

For the dog that has everything, Dog Toys offers breed-specific suggestions on playthings for your pet. The stuffed toys run the gamut from the Launch-A-Ball ($9) to the frivolous Wee Doggie Toy Shoes ($6). Those with a somewhat twisted sense of humor should appreciate the Barnyard Bullies (the Real Mad Cow, the Suspicious Chicken, and the Sheep on the Lamb), as well as the Ex (as in boyfriend). Treats include biscotti, Alaskan salmon ($4), and the like, as well as Hip Chips ($5), for joint pain. Practical items include poop scoopers ($13 and higher), tick removers ($8), and cleaning gloves ($20).

## Doggone Good

(800) 660-2665

www.doggonegood.com

**Payment:** Credit Cards

**Price Range:** $$

This Web site has just about every accessory an agility enthusiast could hope for — the Cabana Crate (starting at $105) is the perfect little tent for any dog in need of a respite. But it offers plenty for else for straight-up dog lovers as well as crossover products that will please both the agility and nonagility set. What dog wouldn't love the jerky Carnivore Cuisine ($9)? Dog lovers will appreciate the dog, bone, and hydrant-shaped cookie cutters, as well as the breed-specific knick knacks, including doormats ($20), painted step stools ($55), and Kung Foo Fido Fortune Cookies ($7). The clothing selection is definitely more for people than dogs, unless you count the Propeller Beanie and Clown Costume.

## Doggon' Wheels

www.doggon.com

**Payment:** Credit Cards

**Price Range:** $$$

What a lifesaver! These custom-designed wheelchairs are well worth the $200-plus when you think about the freedom and mobility they afford disabled pets. Dogs are their biggest users, but they have also created wheelchairs for cats and bunnies. They also offer support slings, booties, and doggie diapers. With a 30-day money-back trial period, you can't lose.

## Dogpark.com

www.dogpark.com

**Payment:** Credit Cards

**Price Range:** $/$$

Dogpark.com's objective is to post a state-by-state reference guide to the nation's dog parks, with all the specifics and particulars: location, hours, water options, poop bags, etc. This ambitious Web site is still in the works, but if you live in

California, you have plenty of parks to choose from. People looking for a pedigree should check out their breed-specific rescue link. And if you and your pup are up for volunteering, check out the Service Dog Organizations link.

## Fat Paddie's Pet Bakery
(214) 553-1100
www.fatpaddies.com
**Payment:** Credit Cards
**Price Range:** $$$

Tired of the usual blah-tasting biscuits inside posh packaging, Fat Paddies focuses on baking, not box decor. All treats are mixed, rolled, and cut by hand, and then baked fresh daily. And with all-natural, human-grade ingredients that are free of sugar, salt, and preservatives, they've been given the stamp of approval by vets. Favorites include Pupcorn Chicken and Chocolate-Flavored Pawsicles. Though Fat Paddie's also carries travel totes, collars, and grooming products, the selling point are the trademark Chicken Lickin' Bisquits.

## Foxy Paws
(866) 406-3699
www.foxypaws.com
**Payment:** Credit Cards
**Price Range:** $$$

Formerly known as Nixon's Top Dog Bakery and Boutique, Foxy Paws stocks the latest in canine couture. If a ballerina dress ($50), a faux fur hoodie ($60), or a bathrobe with rubber duckie appliqués ($20) is de rigueur for your well-dressed dog, then look no further. Foxy also has a great selection of trendy dog carriers (starting at $80) for smaller breeds, in everything from faux crocodile leather to pink plaid, as well as car seats. Collars (starting at $25), dog jewelry, beds, and the perennially posh booties round out the offerings.

## George
(877) 344-5454
www.georgesf.com
**Payment:** Credit Cards
**Price Range:** $$/$$$

This effortlessly hip, eclectic store is for those who prefer their pets' stuff cool, not cutesy. The Stripy Dog Patch Monkey Sweater ($80) is a standout, along with the Oxford Stripe Quilt ($130). With '70s-colored preppy stripes on one side and snugly sherpa on the other, you may want to keep this one for yourself. The Khaki Good Dog Bed ($120 – $200) — definitely more canine cool than shabby chic — will work in just about any room you put it in. Cat offerings include a ticking mattress ($50), fish chips ($4), and organic catnip toys ($8).

## Get Royal Treatment
www.getroyaltreatment.com
**Payment:** Credit Cards
**Price Range:** $$/$$$
If you're unwilling to bask in the dogginess of your pooch, order a supply of fresh currant shampoo ($15) or papaya and aloe wipes ($20). Prince Lorenzo Borghese, grandson of cosmetics queen Princess Marcella Borghese, developed the Royal Treatment line of all-natural, human-grade pet bath and body products as a reaction to his 11-year-old black Lab's "smelling like a dog." In addition, Borghese offers a line of pet treats that includes the Anti-Shed Healthy Coat Treats ($15) and Brusha Brusha Chewy Dental Balls ($20). GRT also carries appropriately regal-looking toile beds ($140 for a medium).

## Glamour Dog
(877) GLAM-DOG
www.glamourdog.com
**Payment:** Credit Cards
**Price Range:** $$$
If you're looking for dog bling, you need look no farther — this online boutique has it all. Designer dog brands include Von Dutch, Juicy, Little Lilly, Hello Kitty, and Puchi Bags, among plenty of other haute-dog must haves. Owner Cindi Whitcher keeps Glamour's shelves filled with over-the-top products like rhinestone-studded collars and leashes, pure silk bandanas, cashmere sweaters, fur-lined boots, and even evening wear. Alongside the extravagances, Glamour Dog also offers dog strollers, pet totes on wheels, and portable pet crates, as well as canine car seats for the practical set.

## Halo, Purely for Pets

(800) 426-4256

www.halopets.com

**Payment:** Credit Cards

**Price Range:** $$$

Halo offers comfort food for pets. Spot's Stew ($45 for a case of 24 cans) — made of slow-cooked chicken and vegetables without any fillers — even looks like people food. You will definitely feel the push for all-natural products from this holistic site, but they also offer affordable supplements (Vita Dreams Daily Greens for $16); healthy treats ($10) in beef, chicken, cod, lamb, and salmon flavor; as well as Dinnery Party powders for those who can't swallow the financial commitment required for the food. If you're willing to do the cooking, Halo has even been known to send out their recipe.

## Harry Barker

(800) HI HARRY

www.harrybarker.com

**Payment:** Credit Cards

**Price Range:** $$$

Enjoy J. Crew–cool offerings from this community-conscious Georgia-based company. From preppy-chic, Chanel-inspired sweaters ($100) to bathrobes ($20), any comfy thing your pet might need for a lazy weekend can be found here. And the porcelain bowls (starting at $14) are refreshingly fun, not fussy. Dog treats ($14), which are free of salt, sugar, and preservatives, come in bacon and peanut butter flavors. Harry's own all-natural shampoos ($14) come in handy for home bathing, with the Prickly Pear Cactus being a safe alternative to flea repellents.

## J. B. Wholesale Pet Supplies, Inc.

(800) 526-0388

www.jbpet.com

**Payment:** Credit Cards

**Price Range:** $/$$/$$$

Luckily for the rest of us, J.B.'s, AKA Bargain Central, is no longer just for New Jersey residents. Clothing options include raincoats (from $6), parkas (from $12), and shearling and faux suede coats ($13). The bed selection is almost endless: tired pooches can get human-grade rest on their Simmons Orthocare beds (the Monarch 7-inch Ortho Bed starts at $60). Cot-style beds, which keep pups' old tired bones off cold, hard floors, start at $35. Other offerings include Adjustable Double Diners (12), ceramic bowls ($7), and basic totes (from $40). All products come with a seven-day guarantee.

## K-9 Top Coat

(888) 833-K9K9

www.K9topcoat.com

**Payment:** Credit Cards

**Price Range:** $$$

A scuba suit for dogs, these Lycra bodysuits can be used to protect your dog from your environment, your environment from your dog, or your dog from himself. The Top Coat has even been featured on *Good Morning America* as a means of reducing dander to help pet-allergy sufferers. The snug-fitting suit (starting at $70) doesn't hamper activity at all, and it's great for bad weather, for allergies, and for covering and protecting injured areas. This canine-conscious company enlisted the help of University of California–Davis to determine whether dogs would overheat in the suit. According to their study, your dog is safe in the Top Coat, in up to 95-degree weather.

## Katie's Kreations

(817) 605-7115

www.katieskreations.net

**Payment:** Credit Cards

**Price Range:** $$$

This online store offers one-stop shopping for everything from customized, cutesy pet gifts (including collar covers, pet wreaths, and holiday-themed gifts) to pet bereavement books. Most gifts can be tailored to fit 50 different breeds of dogs, from Afghan hounds to Yorkshire terriers. Katie's specializes in "Incredible Pettables," stuffed animals that can be delivered with a greeting card ($5 – $50). Katie also offers clothing and pet totes for stuffed animals.

## La Petite Maison

www.lapetitemaison.com
**Payment:** Credit Cards
**Price Range:** $$$

Even though they make more playhouses than doghouses, La
Petite Maison is too fabulous not to list. Forget about dark and
dingy clapboard boxes. These custom-designed doghouses can
be made to match any home and to fit any dog — or you can
choose from one of their designs, including the Swiss Chalet
and French Chateau. Suddenly, being in the doghouse doesn't
seem so bad.

## Max's Closet

(877) 629-9725
www.maxscloset.com
**Payment:** Credit Cards
**Price Range:** $$$

If you want to dress your dog, Max's Closet is the place to find
the clothes. The Paris Chic collection (sweater is $65) would
do Jackie O proud — and even decked in Max's Weekend
Wear (tennis sweaters, $60; striped overalls, $36), your dog
will be dressed to the nines. All of the fashions are inspired,
and modeled, by the eponymous Max, a sweet little Yorkie.
The outfits come in all sizes, but this attire is definitely best left
to delicate dogs.

## Once Upon a Dog

www.onceuponadog.com
**Payment:** Credit Cards
**Price Range:** $$

If you're into alternative, then you've probably heard of
quinoa — the main ingredient in Once upon a Dog's healthy
heart-shaped dog biscuits ($16 for a box). First discovered by
the Incas, quinoa contains as close to perfect a protein balance
as you will get from any common grain. These treats, which
come in two sizes, are a wholesome and tasty option for dogs
with allergies to corn and wheat.

## Original Dog Biscuit

(800) 670-2312

www.originaldogbiscuit.com

**Payment:** Credit Cards

**Price Range:** $$/$$$

These dog biscuits — oatmeal raisin, peanut delight, veggie, and apple crisp ($10 for a one-pound bag) — are so yummy you'll probably want to eat them yourself, which you can since these all-natural organic treats are made with human-grade ingredients. Other treats include Liver Bites ($10 a box) and Diabetic Diet Biscuits ($12 a pound). Supplements include Wild Salmon Oil ($12) and Digestive Enzymes ($11). Frequent buyers get the 13th pound of treats free.

## Orvis Company Store

(800) 541-3541

www.orvis.com

**Payment:** Credit Cards

**Price Range:** $$$

Even though Orvis isn't exclusively for dogs, you can find more here for your pup than at most pooch boutiques, from beds — nesters, bolsters, loungers, and memory foam beds — to tweed coats, reflective vests, and fleece sweaters. And they don't stop there — they also offer tennis ball chuckers, mono-grammed collars, crates, grooming centers, liquid bandages, and vitamins. Call ahead to make sure they have what you are looking for, or you can purchase off the Web site. Look for a new store opening in the Woodlands in summer 2006.

## Patio Park

(877) 206-5946

www.patiopark.com

**Payment:** Credit Cards

**Price Range:** $$$

If you're unable to take your dog outside, bring the outside to your dog with Patio Park ($100). It's a small grass strip with a mock fire hydrant and picket fence. Plastic liners and irrigation strips supposedly make this product safe for use in your home, but you might note that it's not called Living Room Park. The Patio Park makes a lot of sense for injured dogs or people who work odd hours and don't want to walk their dog late at night. Artificial turf ($16) is also available.

## Pet Click

www.petclick.com
**Payment:** Credit Cards
**Price Range:** $$/$$$

All-natural dog food is just a click away on this straightforward Web site. Raw meat, vegetarian, European cuisine — you name it, they stock it. Unless you know your brands and quantities with the raw foods, you'll have to do some research. Fortunately, the customer-service line will answer just about any question you may have. (Canine Caviar Lamb and Pearl Millet Adult Formula is $40 for a 33-pound bag. Steve's Chicken Freeze-Dried Real Food for Dogs is $14 for 7-ounce bag, which translates into about 7 cups of food.)

## Pet Elegance

(800) 942-0742

www.petelegance.com
**Payment:** Credit Cards
**Price Range:** $$$

Fortunately for those of us not living in Portland, this "Bathhouse, Bakery and Boutique" makes its products available via the Internet. They have a rather creative collection of collar designs (from $16): polka dots, daisy, plaid, faux leopard fur, gingham, nautical, and rainbow stripes as well as a specially designed greyhound collar. Tasty treats (12 for $25), including Dogstickers, Bacon Breakfast Croissant Cookies, and Peanut Butter Yogurt Bones, are really healthy and dogs love them.

## Pet Fly's

(818) 558-3597

www.petflys.com
**Payment:** Credit Cards

**Price Range:** $$

If you're looking for street-chic dog carriers, this is the place to go. Approved by most major airlines for cabin travel, the carriers feature wire windows, roll-up flaps, and washable fur-lined bottom inserts. The Curious George carrier starts at $120. Or there's always the Skull and Crossbones carrier for $105.

## Pet Food Direct

www.petfooddirect.com

**Payment:** Credit Cards

**Price Range:** $$/$$$

You won't find too many bargains, but this pet food outlet carries just about every brand of dog food — from the mainstream to the lesser-known all-natural brands. Eight 13.2-ounce cans of Merrick cost $14, and Nature's Logic is $28 for six cans. Check out the pet Travel Central section (click on Specialty Shops) for some great finds. The Outward Hound food bag ($7) makes for easy transport of all your dog's dining essentials. They also have a large selection of poop-removal products (scoop/rake combos from $12) that make this stinky task a little less unpleasant.

## Petography/Jim Dratfield

(800) 738-6472

www.petography.com

**Hours:** By Appt

**Payment:** Credit Cards, Checks

**Price Range:** $$$

Whether it means singing an aria to an Italian greyhound, doing Kabuki for a Japanese chin, or dancing a jig for an Irish wolfhound, Jim will do whatever it takes to make your pet picture-perfect. He is used to working with untrained animals, and says the most difficult dog is still easier to photograph than the best cat. He's had several books published: *The Quotable Canine, The Quotable Feline, Pug Shots,* and *Underdogs: Beauty Is More Than Just Fur Deep.* And Jim's photography has received raves in all the right magazines. For the person who has everything, Petography may be the perfect gift. (Call for pricing.)

## Planet Dog

(800) 381-1516

www.planetdog.com

**Payment:** Credit Cards

**Price Range:** $$/$$$

For the Earth-minded pooch, it doesn't get any better than Planet Dog. The Planet is best known for Solar System Balls, which include the Orbo with Treat Spot (from $6). The super-padded canvas beds are comfy from the start, while the hemp collars ($14) will only get softer and prettier with time. The matching Weekend Food Bag ($15) and Travel Food and Water Bowl ($8) are musts for pup-toting travelers. And dog-o-philes will appreciate the white T-shirts emblazoned with "Got Woof" and "Who's Your Doggie."

## Purely Pets

(804) 748-7626

www.purelypets.com

**Payment:** Credit Cards

**Price Range:** $$$

If you're on the verge of going holistic, Purely Pets will definitely pave the way. Beginners can get their feet wet with the all-natural dry foods, while the more advanced can try out some of their shared recipes. The products are indexed by brand, by ailments, and from A to Z — which makes searching a bit of a challenge. Searching by manufacturer is usually the simplest. Pet nutritionist and Purely Pets founder Darleen Rudnick is available for consultation via phone or the Purely Pets private chat room — the cost is $50. If that's too steep, you can always take advantage of the articles on the site (click on Wellness Center).

## Ruff Wear

www.ruffwear.com

**Payment:** Credit Cards

**Price Range:** $$/$$$

Billed as gear for dogs on the go, Ruff Wear provides boots ($38), collapsible bowls with cinch tops (starting at $15),

packs, and float coats ($50) for the active dog. If your idea of
a trail hike involves back-country passes and bear bags, then
this Web site can outfit your dog accordingly. For instance,
you can order a W.A.G. bag, or a Mutt Hutt ($98) — modeled
on your own high-tech tent, but with a doggie door for night-
time nature calls.

## Sit Stay

(800) SIT-STAY

www.sitstay.com

**Payment:** Credit Cards

**Price Range:** $$/$$$

This one-stop dog-product site is filled with a wide array
of items — from figurines that your grandmother would
love to cocktail-cool dog-bone-shaped ice cube trays. Dogs
respond well to the Bow Wow Botanicals Chinese formulas
— Mellow Dog ($8) is served treat-style, so there's no added
pill-administering stress. The Chirobed ($116) is great for
older dogs, while the Comfort Pup Bed ($30) provides your
new puppy with a stuffed-animal bed, complete with
electronic heartbeat to help ease the transition.

## Tails by the Lake

www.tailsbythebay.com

**Payment:** Credit Cards

**Price Range:** $$$

Formerly known as Tails by the Bay, this site is tops for top-
of-the-line clothes, furnishings, and gifts. Beds range from the
artist's loft-hip Hydrant Dog Mat ($95) to the mod Bowhaus Pet
Crate (from $425). Pet-toting equipment includes the outdoorsy
All Terrain Pet Stroller ($285), the super-swanky Spice Puchi
bag ($390), and the I-Want-A-Baby Snuggly Sacks ($35). Other
offerings include the Dog Bike Seat ($85) and the Outdoor
Sleeping Bag ($85).

## Taj Ma Hound, The

(866) 426-0980

www.tajmahound.com

**Payment:** Credit Cards, Checks

**Price Range:** $$

From Special Occasion Bones ($14) to Epetcurian specialities (starting at $4), your dog can now say "bone appetite," thanks to Krista Aversano and Jake Karmin. Disappointed with the stale, chemical-drenched treats in standard pet and grocery stores, they began making high-quality natural products in their kitchen, and taste-tested the goodies on their own pup.

## Three Dog Bakery

(800) 4TREATS

www.threedog.com

**Payment:** Credit Cards

**Price Range:** $/$$/$$$

Three Dog Bakery, with stores popping up all over the country, is tops for healthy, yummy dog treats. Their online Dogalog has some great offerings, including Gift Boxers (from $23), Monthly Dogliveries ($17), and custom-made cakes ($20). And if you want to treat your canine to some home cooking, get the *Three Dog Bakery Cookbook*.

## Trixie & Peanut

www.trixieandpeanut.com

**Payment:** Credit Cards

**Price Range:** $$$

As much fun to browse as it is to buy from, this site has every-thing from basic balls to lavish pet carriers (the Bree Basket Pet Tote is $185) and clothing. If you're in the market for Nail Pawlish or a bridesmaid dress ($118) for your pampered pooch, check out this Web site. Beds range from the mod BowHaus pet crate ($399) to the perfect Sniffany & Co. bed ($129). Trixie founder Susan Bing is a graphic designer, and it shows. The site is easy to navigate and products are clearly displayed.

## Uptown Pets

www.uptownpets.com
**Payment:** Credit Cards
**Price Range:** $$$
If you want to deck out your conservative canine, this Burberry-filled site is a good place to start. Burberry coats (from $90) are an instant classic. Other offerings include the Furcedes Bed (from $250, it's the only way for the sports-car set to go); tiaras (from $20), perfect for pup princesses; and the ultra-hip Wetnoz bowl collection (individual pieces from $30).

## Waggin' Tails

www.waggintails.com
**Payment:** Credit Cards
**Price Range:** $$
All sorts of all-natural remedies here — from dental care to treats (*Chicken Soup* . . . treats start at $5) to the ultimate hair remover, Kong Zoom Groom ($9). They also tell you which breeds the individual products work best on. The Buddy Bowl (starting at $13) is as spillproof a bowl as you will find, making it great for the car. Plus, they carry several brands and varieties of all-natural dog food, including Merrick ($13 for twelve 5.5-ounce servings).

## Wagwear

www.wagwear.com
**Payment:** Credit Cards
**Price Range:** $$$
Casual cool goes cutting-edge with Wagwear's simple textures and color combinations that define urban chic. A merino wool sweater ($80) comes in orange and gray, citrus and gray, and navy blue and gray. You will definitely want to get the fabulous shearling-lined suede collar (from $40) and matching leash (from $68) — you'll love how it looks and your dog will love how it feels. With the safari-chic cotton ripstop carrier ($208), your dog will have his own little totable tent.

# Dog Rescue Directory

There are numerous pet-rescue groups in Philadelphia. All of them are to be commended for the work they do, not only to rescue animals from euthanasia but also to place them in loving homes. Regretfully, there is not enough space to list all of these groups.

Additionally, there are SPCA and Humane Society shelters listed in the next section under Lost Dog Help. All are worth checking out, although some are a bit more intense to visit than others.

If you are not up for a trip to the shelter, be aware that when you adopt an animal from a rescue group, you make it possible for them to rescue another animal from a shelter!

Whatever you decide to do, please, please do not purchase a pet from a pet store. Almost all of those precious little puppies are products of puppy mills. And as long as people continue to purchase animals from pet stores, those puppy mills will stay in business. Furthermore, there are way too many phenomenal homeless dogs — of all shapes, sizes, ages and breeds — that not only deserve loving homes but also would make outstanding pets.

If you like a particular breed, many of the pet-rescue super-sites have links to purebred dog-rescue sites. And if you have your heart set on getting a puppy, there are usually a few to choose from, in both the shelters and the rescue groups.

## Animal Rescue, Inc.

(717) 993-3232
2 Heritage Farm Dr
(@ Harris Mill Rd #3)
New Freedom, PA  17349
www.animalrescueinc.org
**Hours:** Mon 1 AM – 4 PM
       Wed 12 PM – 2 PM
       Sat – Sun 1 AM – 4 PM
**Payment:** Credit Cards
**Price Range:** $$$

Open the gate to visit this rural animal shelter and a pack of happy dogs will race to greet you. Just a short drive past the Maryland/Pennsylvania state line, Grace Froelich's bucolic 33-acre farm is a no-kill rescue shelter where dogs are allowed to run free in fenced-in fields. Open since 1976, the shelter offsets costs by charging a $125 adoption fee. Animal Rescue, Inc. has another location in Baltimore that is a strictly a cattery.

## Francisvale Home for Smaller Animals

(610) 688-1018
P.O. Box 282
Wayne, PA  19087
www.francisvale.org
**Hours:** Wed – Tue 9:30 AM – 3 PM
       Sun 11 AM – 3 PM
       Sat – Thu 9:30 AM – 3 PM
**Payment:** Free
**Price Range:** $

Orphaned or abandoned pets are lucky to get a berth in this small, volunteer-run, no-kill shelter that provides a safe haven for unwanted senior animals. If you're thinking of taking one of these dogs home, be prepared to provide a personal and veterinary reference, and undergo a home inspection. The basic adoption fee is $45. At the on-site pet cemetary, visit the grave of Francis, the pup after which this shelter was named. According to legend, Dr. and Mrs. George McClellan found him shivering and homeless one snowy night over a century ago, and were inspired to save legions of others like him. Parking lot located on Arden Road.

## Friends of Camden Animal Shelter (FOCAS) Animal Adoption Center

(856) 435-9116
501 N Berlin Rd, (@ Shady Side Ave)
Lindenwold, NJ 8021
www.animaladoption.com
**Hours:** Mon – Wed 1 AM – 6 PM, Thu 1 AM – 8 PM,
Fri – Sat 9 AM – 8 PM, Sun 1 AM – 6 PM
**Payment:** Checks
**Price Range:** $

You won't find dogs sitting around here, panting to be adopted; they're too busy making people smile. Through this shelter's Pet Therapy Program, dogs visit with people in hospitals, nursing homes, and retirement facilities. The shelter also plays matchmaker, placing gentle, older dogs and cats with appropriate seniors. This group's serious commitment to animal welfare and community education results in thousands of adoptions annually. Ninety percent of the funds donated to this no-kill shelter go directly to the animals, providing them with food, medical care, and shelter. The adoption fee is $125 for puppies; $100 for dogs. A completed application and references are required. Check their Web site for events like the popular holiday soiree.

## Main Line Rescue

(610) 337-9225
www.mainlinerescue.com
**Hours:** By Appt
**Payment:** Free

Main Line Rescue takes in abandoned, abused, and neglected animals and places them in foster care. While they are being nurtured back to health by volunteers, the pups do their own volunteering, providing love and affection to hospital patients and residents of assisted-living homes through pet-therapy programs. You can check out pics of these four-legged community activists on the group's Web site. Dogs can be seen by appointment only, usually in the evening. All animals are vaccinated and neutered/spayed prior to being placed in homes. Only after a careful screening process — in which Main Line Rescue makes sure you have a fenced-in yard, among other things — can you take your dog home.

# Puppy Starter Kit

## DOG LICENSING

You are required to get your dog licensed.

The easiest way to get a dog license is to download the form off the Internet.

You will also need to pull together a few documents before animal control will issue you a dog license. Policies vary from county to county, but they all require the following:

A) A copy of your dog's current rabies vaccination certificate
B) A copy of your dog's spay or neuter certificate (for a discount)
C) A check or money order — expect to pay more if you haven't gotten your dog spayed or neutered

Following is a list of agencies (with Web site addresses) where you can get a dog license throughout the Greater Philadelphia area.

**Please note:** If you are a resident of a city that does not fall under the jurisdiction of animal control for your county, you can usually obtain a license online from your city's Web site.

### Philadelphia
http://www.phila.gov/health/units/ehs/petlicense.html

If you can provide proof from your vet that your dog has been microchipped, you can get a permanent dog tag.

## Bucks County

www.buckscounty.org
Click on link for *Government*
Under Row Officers, click on link for *Treasurer*
Click on link for *dog license*

## Chester County

http://dsf.chesco.org
Click on *Services*
From drop-down menu, click on *Dog Licenses*

## Delaware County

www.co.delaware.pa.us/treasurer/dog.html

## Montgomery County

www.montcopa.org
Click on link for *Departments*
Click on link for *Treasurer*
Click on link for *Dogs*

## Delaware State

https://egov.dnrec.state.de.us
Click on link for *Dog Licenses*

## Trenton, New Jersey

Residents of Trenton, NJ, must show up in person to obtain a dog license.

Office of Vital Statistics
City Hall
(609) 989-3236
319 E State St
Trenton, NJ 08608

# SPAYING & NEUTERING

## THE TOP REASONS TO SPAY/NEUTER YOUR DOG:

- Spaying and neutering helps reduce the animal-population problem
- Spayed/neutered animals live up to three years longer than their unaltered counterparts
- Spaying your female dog before her first estrus cycle greatly reduces her chances of getting breast cancer and eliminates the possibility of uterine and ovarian cancers
- Neutering your dog will make him less aggressive than non-neutered males
- Neutering your dog will make him less likely to roam/run away than if he were unaltered
- Neutering your dog will make him less likely to bite — the majority of dog bites come from unaltered males
- If you remain unconvinced, think about this:
  Each year 8 million animals are euthanized because they do not have homes

*By spaying/neutering your dog, you are doing your part to help curb the pet overpopulation crisis.*

If you adopted your dog from a local SPCA or rescue group, he or she will most likely already be neutered or spayed. If your dog has not been altered, talk to your vet about when you should spay/neuter your dog.

If you cannot afford the cost of spaying/neutering your dog, contact the Alliance for Philadelphias Animals at www.animalalliancepa.org.

# Lost Dog Help

Having a pet disappear is a very scary thing. However, there are some immediate steps you can take that will significantly increase the chances of their safe return. This section includes a list of suggestions to get you started on your search, as well as a list of local shelters and resources.

- Stay calm and make a plan.
- Enlist the help of as many people as possible.
- Delegate as many tasks as possible.
- Divide up the areas then fan out and search the streets.
- Call, or have someone else call, vets and animal hospitals in the area.
- Make, or have someone else make, flyers that include the following:
    1) A picture, preferably a color copy, of your pet.
    2) Identifying characteristics, such as age, weight and markings.
    3) State that your pet needs medication. (Some people believe that if you state this, your pet is more likely to be returned.)
    4) The offering of a monetary reward for the return of your pet.
- Go, or send someone, to the shelters:
    1) Look through all of the kennels for your dog.
    2) Show pictures/flyers to the staff and volunteers.
    3) Post flyers on the bulletin board(s).
- Check, or have someone check, posted pictures of found dogs on shelter and dog-rescue organization Web sites. If you spot your dog:
    1) Copy down the identification/impound number posted with your dog's picture.
    2) Call the shelter:
        a) Give them the identification/impound number.
        b) Ask them what proof of ownership you need to show them.
    3) Go immediately (or as soon as they open) to the shelter to collect your dog and take him home.

- If you do not find your dog's picture posted on a shelter Web site, he may still be there. Return to the shelters at least every few days to look for him.
- Post flyers or signs in the following places:
    1) Local shelters.
    2) Veterinarians' offices, animal hospitals and animal-emergency clinics.
    3) Grooming salons.
    4) Pet-supply stores.
    5) Dog parks.
    6) Anywhere that dog-conscious people might frequent, such as neighborhood coffee shops, bookstores, etc.
- Consider hiring a "pet detective."

## Philadelphia

### Philadelphia Animal Care and Control Association
(215) 685-9057
111-131 West Hunting Park Aves
Philadelphia, PA 19140
www.phila.gov/health/pacca
**Hours:** 24/7

## Chester County

### Chester County SPCA
(610) 692-6113
1212 Phoenixville Pk
(between Boot Rd & Rte 100)
West Chester, PA 19380
www.ccspca.org
**Hours:** Mon, Thu 11 AM – 6:45 PM
Tue – Wed, Fri 11 AM – 4:15 PM
Sat – Sun 11 AM – 4:15 PM

## Delaware County

# Delaware County SPCA

(610) 566-1370
555 Sandy Bank Rd
(off Rte. 1, between Rte 252 & Old State Rd)
Media, PA  19063
www.delcospca.org
**Hours:** Mon – Sat 10 AM – 10 PM
　　　 SUN 10 AM – 3 PM

## Montgomery County

# Montgomery County SPCA

www.montgomerycountyspca.org
**Hours:** Mon – Fri 11AM to 4:30 PM
　　　 Sat 10 AM – 3 PM
　　　 Sun 12 PM – 3 PM

### Abington Shelter

(215) 886-8802
1006 Edge Hill Road
(between Easton & Susquehanna Rds)
Roslyn, PA 19001

### Conshohocken Shelter

(610) 825-0111
19 E Ridge Pike
(between Butler Pk & Spring Mill Rd)
Conshohocken, PA 19428

### Perkiomenville Shelter

(610) 754-7822
1059 Sweifford Road
(between Little & Yost Rds)
Perkiomenville, PA 18074

# Bucks County

## Bucks County SPCA
(215) 794-7425
1665 Street Road
(between Pineville & Stoney Hill Rds)
Lahaska, PA  18938
www.bcspca.org
**Hours:** Mon, Wed – Sat: 10:00 AM – 4:00 PM
       Tue – 10:00 AM – 7:00 PM

# Delaware State

## Delaware SPCA
(302) 998-2281
455 Stanton Christiana Rd
(between Ogletown Stanton & Churchmans Rds)
Newark, DE  19713
www.delspca.org
**Hours:** Mon – Fri. 10 AM – 5 PM, Sat 10 AM – 3 PM

## Delaware Humane Association
(302) 571-0111
701 A St
(between Walnut & Buttonwood Sts)
Wilmington, DE 19801
www.dehumane.org
**Hours:** Tue – Fri 12 PM – 7 PM
       Sat – Sun 11 AM – 4 PM

# New Jersey

## Trenton Animal Shelter
(609) 989-3254
72 Escher St
(off Southard St)
Trenton, NJ
www.petfinder.com/shelters/tas.html
**Hours:** Mon – Fri 1 PM – 3 PM
       Sat – Sun By Appt

# When Dogs Go To Heaven

The disparity between our pets' lifespan and our own is one of the great injustices in this world. Losing a pet is a very sad, sometimes devastating, experience. Many people do not realize how much they will be affected until it happens. If you are too overcome with grief to deal with the logistics, many veterinarians' offices will take care of everything for you, including picking up your pet and having him cremated or buried. It may seem like a morbid thing to do, but it might be a good idea to ask your vet in advance what their policies are. Then, when the need arises, you will know whether you can count on them and what to expect.

If you prefer to take care of everything yourself, this section contains information, listed in the order it is most frequently needed:

## EUTHANASIA

The decision to put an animal to sleep is one of the most difficult decisions a person must make. The fact that it may be the most compassionate thing to do does not make it any easier. You may want to consult with your vet, and perhaps someone else that you trust, and ask them to help you determine if it is the right time and the right thing to do for your pet.

If you decide euthanasia is the best thing to do, you may want to arrange for a vet come to your house. This way, your dog can spend his final moments in the comfort of his home. Ask your vet to prescribe a sedative for your dog that you can give him prior to your vet's arrival. If your vet will not perform in-home euthanasia, ask him or her for a recommendation of someone who provides this service.

# FINAL ARRANGEMENTS

A reputable pet funeral home or crematorium should treat you
and your dog with compassion and respect as well as provide
you with options that fit your financial situation. You may want
to make arrangements in advance so when the time comes,
you will not have to worry about deciding what to do.

## Brickhaven Pet Burials

(215) 785-1766
610 New Rodgers Rd
(off Rte 413)
Bristol, PA  19007
**Hours:** By Appt
**Payment:** Credit Cards, Checks
**Price Range:**  $$$
For more than 30 years, Beverly Brick has been helping
people say goodbye to their beloved pets. An avid animal
lover, Beverly at one time owned 17 dogs, as well as a few
cats, birds, and fish. Offering airtight, water-sealed pet caskets
 for burial in addition to cremation services, she and her
partner, Denise, prepare animals for the afterlife with respect
and compassion. Hosted viewing services at the facility can
accommodate up to 30 people. Cremations start at $275 for an
animal up to 30 pounds; burials range from $500 to $1,000.
Brickhaven is available to serve you 24/7, including holidays.

## Paws to Heaven

(215) 744-4400
Frankford Arsenal Business Center
5301 Tacony Street, #143
Philadelphia, PA 19137
**Hours:** By Appt
**Payment:** Credit Cards, Checks
**Price Range:** $$/$$$
Paws offers private and group cremation, and even allows
people to be present while their pet is cremated. Alternatively,
if the entire process is too upsetting to even think about, they
will handle everything through your vet. They will pick up
animals from veterinary clinics/animal hospitals or a person's
home. The ashes will be returned to you (or the vet) in a cedar
box, within five days. They also offer a selection of somewhat
ornate urns.

## PET LOSS — BOOKS

### Coping with Sorrow on the Loss of Your Pet
by Moira Anderson, 2nd ed. Alpine Publications 1996

### Coping with the Loss of a Pet: A Gentle Guide for All Who Love a Pet
by Christina M. Lemieux, Ph.D., Wallace R. Clark & Co. 1988

### The Loss of a Pet
by Wallace Sife, Ph.D., rev. ed. NY Howell Book House 1998

### Pet Loss: A Thoughtful Guide for Adults and Children
by Herbert Nieberg, Ph.D., Harper & Row 1996

## PET LOSS HOTLINES

### ASPCA NATIONAL PET LOSS HOTLINE
**Hours:** 24/7
**Counselors:** Volunteers
**Phone:** (800) 946-4646 press 140 7211 and then enter your phone number
**E-mail:** stephaniel@aspca.org

### University of Illinois, College of Veterinary Medicine: C.A.R.E. Helpline for Companion Animal Related Emotions
**Hours:** Tues/Thurs 7 PM – 9 PM CST
**Counselors:** Volunteer veterinary students
**Hotline:** (217) 244-2273
**E-mail:** brannan@vivc.edu.

### University of California, Davis School of Veterinary Medicine: Pet Loss Support Hotline
**Hours:** Mon – Fri 6:30 PM – 9:30 PM PST
**Counselors:** Trained volunteers
**Hotline:** (800) 565-1526

## Companion Animal Association of Arizona Inc.: Pet Grief Support Service

**Hours:** 24/7
**Counselors:** Trained volunteers
**Hotline:** (602) 995-5885*
**Office Phone:** (602) 258-3306*
**Additional Services:** support groups, literature
*Long distance calls returned collect

## Cornell University, College of Veterinary Medicine: Pet Loss Support Hotline

**Hours:** Tues – Thurs 6 PM – 9 PM EST
**Counselors:** Trained volunteers
**Hotline:** (607) 253-3932
**Web site:** www.vet.cornell.edu/public/petloss/

## Michigan State University, College of Veterinary Medicine: Pet Loss Support Program

**Hours:** Tues – Thurs 6:30 PM – 9:30 PM EST
**Counselors:** Volunteer veterinary students
**Hotline:** (517) 353-5064
**E-mail:** Walshaw@pilot.msu.edu
**Additional Services:** monthly support groups

## Tufts University, Cummings School of Veterinary Medicine: Pet Loss Support Hotline

**Hours:** Mon – Fri 6 PM – 9 PM EST
**Counselors:** Trained volunteers
**Hotline:** (508) 839-7966
**Web site:** www.tufts.edu/vet/petloss/

# PET LOSS RESOURCES ON THE WEB

## The Association for Pet Loss and Bereavement
**Phone:** (718) 382-0960
**Web site:** www.aplb.org
**Services:** Chat rooms, nationwide database that includes pet cemeteries, lawyers specializing in pet-related wrongful-action cases, as well as hotline, counselor, and support group information

## Grief Healing
**Web site:** www.griefhealing.com
**Services:** General loss as well as pet-loss resource, tips for helping children cope, links

## Rainbow Bridge
**Web site:** www.rainbowbridge.com
**E-mail**: friends@rainbowsbridge.com
**Services:** Pet-loss forums, questions to help you work through your grief, chat rooms, one-on-one counseling, tributes, euthanasia advice, virtual memorial ($25), tips for helping children cope, links

## Delta Society
**Web site:** www.deltasociety.org
**Services:** List of Web sites, hotlines, counselors, and support groups

## SUPPORT GROUPS/COUNSELORS
### Chester, Delaware and Mongtomery Counties

**Flack, Christine R. M.A.** Cognitive-Behavioral Therapist specializing in Pet Bereavement
**Phone:** (610) 695-8821
**E-mail:** zendog2000@email.msn.com
**Services:** Counseling in Malvern area (call for address)

## Peterson, Linda M. LSW
## Center for Pet Loss Counseling and Education

**Phone:** (610) 399-3168

**Services:** counseling, support group in Chadds Ford area (call for address)

## Susan D. Rappaport, MSW, LSW
## CARES (Center for Animal Referral and Emergency Services)

2010 Cabot Boulevard West, Suite D
Langhorne, PA 19047

**Phone:** (215) 292-1057

**Services:** counseling, support group (meetings held Monday nights, 6 PM – 7 PM, $35 per session)

# Index

# C

# D